OHIO'S
INDIAN PAST

BY
LAR HOTHEM

ISBN   0-9317041-7-9

Additional copies of this book may be ordered for $14.95 plus $2.00 p&h from the publisher at the below address. Ohio residents, please include appropriate sales tax.

Hothem House
PO Box 458
Lancaster, OH 43130

Contents

5

OHIO TIME FRAME

PALEO　　　　14,000 BC　—　8000 BC

ARCHAIC　　　8000 BC　—　1000 BC

WOODLAND　　1000 BC　—　AD 800

MISSISSIPPIAN　AD 800　—　AD 1650

Please note: These times are general, not definitive. There was some overlapping of time periods, just as there was some cultural carryover from one period to another.

INTRODUCTION

Of all the Midwestern states, Ohio probably has the greatest number of amateur archaeologists and collectors—those who have studied the region's prehistoric past and have gathered up bits of cultural debris. This tradition goes back into the late 1800s, when scientists like McLean, Read and Shepherd investigated early Ohio sites. They were followed in the early 1900s by such luminaries as Fowke and Moorehead. All these gentlemen, especially Warren K. Moorehead, turned out books and other writings that were popular in their day and are still of value to modern students.

The state of Ohio is rich in prehistoric cultures or lifeways, and the artifacts created by these ancient peoples exist in the uncounted millions. The earliest Paleo people produced matchless projectile points, while the Archaic period had axes, points and knives, bannerstones and more. At least three Woodland groups put up mounds, great piles of earth or stones that are still impressive today. The Mississippian time-frame had fine pottery and celts, distinctive arrowheads and knives. Almost anywhere one looked in Ohio one could find the remains of ancient villages and camp-sites, earthworks and trails.

All this encouraged the search for knowledge, often in the form of whatever artifacts could be picked up before they were broken by the plow or buried forever by construction. For generations farmers tilling the land have been drawn to the mysterious objects left behind by vanished races, the curious "Indian stones" that ended up stored in attics or sheds or tool-boxes. Archaeologists, both amateur and professional, have gone to existing sites and tried to piece together what life was like dozens of centuries ago. Where the ancients lived was easy enough to determine; how they lived is a story that has not yet been fully told.

In the course of research on various projects the author has located interesting and often little-publicized information and facts about Ohio's Indian and archaeological past. The information is put forth here, along with photographs of artifacts done in flint, hardstone and slate. This gives an idea of the scope and great amount of work that has already been done in the state, as well as what remains to be done.

For example: Why have no Early Paleo kill-sites been found in the Ohio, when they almost certainly are present? How was the lifeway the same and different between Late Paleo and Early Archaic peoples in Ohio, and where and when did these lifeways converge or overlap? In other words, why did two different cultural patterns exist at the same time, if only briefly?

What was the Middle Archaic all about and what are the real differences between the Late Archaic and the Early Woodland? What happened to the Middle Woodland Hopewell peoples? Why is so little known about the Late Woodland Intrusive Mound people, and others who coexisted at the time? How did the Mississippian-era cultures differ along the Ohio River and just south of the shores of Lake Erie?

Work and study have gone on with varying levels of intensity for nearly 150 years, all in an effort to comprehend the human story of ancient Ohio. If the long-ago inhabitants of what is now a modern state could see how avidly their traces are sought and how carefully their works are preserved, one wonders what their feelings would be. Probably they would be somewhat puzzled, even amused. And perhaps they would be pleased, for they are being remembered in a respectful and honorable way. They will never be forgotten.

Lar Hothem – July 26, 1996 – Lancaster, Ohio

PRIME ARTIFACT REGION

While many Ohio counties are rich in prehistoric artifacts—Coshocton and Ross, to name just two—one three-county region has produced a wide variety of high-grade pieces. This is the area surrounding Buckeye Lake, which was created to feed a canal system and was formerly the location of the Great Swamp. The Lake itself includes parts of northeastern Fairfield, northwestern Perry, and southern Licking Counties. In fact, some experienced surface-hunters have said the Buckeye Lake region has been the most productive of any in Ohio. Such artifacts were surface-found and they include most raw materials and all time-periods. (Hothem, Lar, various sources)

PALEO POINT DISTRIBUTION

There are general distribution areas for Paleo period artifacts in Ohio. "...the pooled series of all Paleo Indian point types followed two interrelated patterns of distribution. One, that the maximum distribution of points follows a diagonal line across the state from southwest to northeast, corresponding roughly to the maximum Wisconsin glacial boundary. The second line of distribution... follows the Great Miami and Scioto Rivers, two of the three major tributaries of the Ohio River." (Graham, Paul B., "General Overview of Aboriginal Culture History in Ohio," *Ohio Archaeologist*, Vol. 33 No. 2, Spring 1983, p 11)

STONE BOWL FINDS

Very few stone bowls or well-made stone containers have been found in Ohio. One, however, did come from Mound No. 33, Hopewell Mound Group, Ross County. "As to the stone bowl... I cannot give the exact measurements from memory, but the statement that it is about 12 or 13 pounds in weight, cut out from solid lime-stone, 1¼ of an inch thick, 5 inches deep, and 14½ inches in diameter will vary only a trifle from the truth. It is strangely of the type of bowls found on the Pacific

Coast and nothing like it has ever been discovered in our Ohio Valley Mounds." (Moorehead, Warren K., "The Hopewell Group," *The Antiquarian*, Vol. 1 Part 8, August 1897, p 213)

INDIAN FOOD SOURCES

An idea of what late prehistoric peoples would have likely lived on in Ohio can be gained from the below facts, subject of course to slight adjustments allowed for improved research since the original source was compiled. The state has about 2500 plant life species, 60 of mammals, and 358 species of birds of which 181 nest in Ohio. (WPA Writer's Program, *The Ohio Guide*, 1940, p 5)

TALLY-MARK THEORIES

Tally-marks (once thought to represent counting) are short and narrow lines, usually spaced equidistant on the edges of artifacts. These were sometimes placed on Late Archaic birdstones. For whatever reason(s), such marks were most frequently done on a specimen that was broken or damaged. There is some thought that the marks might simply be decorative or that some sort of magical healing or fixing of the broken artifact took place. (Hothem, Lar, various sources)

CIRCLEVILLE EARTHWORKS

While most students of Ohio archaeology are aware that Circleville was named after a large Hopewell earthwork in the form of a circle, lesser-known is the fact that the circle joined, via a gateway, a large square. This was precisely 55 rods or 907½ feet per side. The walls of the square were about ten feet high, and there were eight gateways or openings in the walls, these being at mid-length and at the corners. Exactly opposite each opening a small mound was located. Portions of the wall were removed to make bricks. (Atwater, Caleb, *Description of Antiquities Discovered in the State of Ohio and Other Western States*, 1820, pp 141-143)

EGGS FOR ARTIFACTS

Years ago there were unusual (and today highly protected) items that were traded for prehistoric artifacts, some of which likely were taken from Ohio. "I have eggs of the Great Horned and Barred owl, and Red Tailed and Coopers hawk to exchange for good Indian relics or good scientific books. Eggs guaranteed A No. 1. Jasper Brown, Norway, Ia." (Advertisement, *The Archaeologist*, Vol. 2 No. 2, February 1894)

WOODLAND PERIOD CACHES

Regarding cache finds of Woodland-era leaf-shaped blades in Ohio, a large number were recovered from wetland areas, especially when low-lying sections were drained for agricultural purposes. These areas in many cases seem to have once been lakes, ponds and swamps, and were purposely sought out as the places to deposit large numbers of artifacts. It is somewhat of a mystery why this is so, since it would seem that higher ground would be just as suitable and appropriate. There are two possible explanations, however. One is practical, in that several flint-knappers have stated that damp flint or flint retaining original water chips better than flint that has a very low moisture content. Another reason may simply be added security, in that the cache would not likely be dug up by accident in ancient times. Also, it would be difficult to trail the person or persons placing the artifacts or locate the cache by disturbed or settled earth. And, in water, the scent of people placing the artifacts could not be picked up by tracking dogs. Actually, from the rather shallow depth of some of the caches—and the fact that they were sometimes placed in containers—the artifacts may simply have been placed on the pond or lake bottom where they would have been easy to retrieve. Eventually of course the artifacts were gradually covered by the erosion silt and decayed vegetation of centuries. This matter of leaf-shaped caches certainly deserves additional study. (Hothem, Lar, various sources)

PREHISTORIC ENCLOSURES

Of the classic hilltop enclosures that follow the natural topography of the site, a primary example is Ft. Ancient in Warren County, Ohio. Most geometric enclosures on level or near-level lands are in Butler, Licking and Ross Counties and others adjacent to the Miami, Muskingum and Scioto Rivers. There are also enclosures that combine characteristics of the two just-noted earthwork types, and these are mainly in southern Ohio and in several counties adjoining Lake Erie. (Mills, William C., *Archeological Atlas Of Ohio*, 1914, pp III-IV)

COPPER EFFIGY

Early announcements in the form of advertisements are fascinating today; in this case one wonders about the real story. "Ancient copper idol found on shores of Lake Erie. Very singular. Will send photograph of it. Worth $100. Price $20. Barton Walters, Circleville, Ohio." (Advertisement, "Exchange Department," *The Archaeologist*, Vol. 3 No. 5, May 1895, p 177)

POINTS SOUTH

Some interesting early thoughts (now largely ignored) are represented in these comments: "...nothing is more striking in regard to the relics of the Ohio mounds than their southern origin. Much the larger portion, in numbers, were from southern waters. ...Besides, how could the rich valleys of the lower streams with their milder climate have failed to attract settlement when they could be reached from the north simply by committing themselves in primitive canoes to the current of the great streams?" (Walker, C. B., *The Mississippi Valley and Prehistoric Events*, 1880, p 138)

PALEO POINT LENGTHS

Fluted and lanceolate Paleo points from Ohio have a slight size difference of one-fifth inch, at least in a large sample that was taken. Of the Ohio Historical Society's collection numbers (lanceolates, 215; fluted 140), lanceolates averaged 2.9 inches, while fluted points averaged 3.1 inches. (Shetrone, Henry C., "The Folsom Phenomena As Seen From Ohio," *Ohio Archaeological & Historical Society Publications*, Vol. XLV, 1936, pp 254-255)

SPRUCE HILL

The "Ancient Stone Work" near Bourneville, Ross County, now known as Spruce Hill, may be the largest such hilltop enclosure in North America in terms of acreage enclosed. Located southwest of Chillicothe (with Paint Creek just to the west), the walls total about 2¼ miles and surround about 140 acres. The walls line the edges of a steep hill with a plain-like top, in which were located several small stone mounds. A water-filled depression or pond of about two acres in size was "…adequate to the wants of a thousand head of cattle." (Squier, Ephraim G. and E. H. Davis, *Ancient Monuments of the Mississippi Valley*, 1848, pp 11-13)

GORGET NAME

Flat-faced gorgets of slate were once known as "whetstones" to some Ohio farmers. No doubt this was due to a similarity to typical rural sharpening stones. (Vietzen, Raymond C., *Ancient Man in Northern Ohio*, 1941, p 16)

MOUND BASEMENT

At times prehistoric works have been used for different purposes in more modern times. "In March, 1870, a mound measuring, after being much reduced by plowing, fourteen feet in height by seventy feet in diameter, was partially explored in the corporate limits of Mount Vernon, Ohio. …[Also found were] a number of perforated, finely polished slate ornaments and pendants, several polished celts, and more than two hundred arrow and spear heads of fine workmanship. These are now in the possession of Mr. Rogers whose house stands on the mount — the excavation of 25 by 35 feet being utilized for a cellar." (Mills, William C., "Recent Discoveries," *The Archaeologist*, Vol. 3 No. 2, February 1895, p 73)

OHIO MOUND NUMBERS

Varying numbers of prehistoric earthworks have been computed for Ohio. "In the 1880s it was estimated that there were ten thousand mounds and one thousand earth-walled enclosures in southern Ohio, the great majority of them relics of the Mound Builders. In Ross County... there were five hundred mounds and one hundred large walled enclosures." (Hyde, George E., *Indians of the Woodlands*, 1975, p 28)

ROLLER PESTLES

Very little is known about roller pestles in Ohio, and they are concisely described in the following words: "The roller pestles were cylindrical in form; usually tapering slightly from the center to the ends; varying in length from 22 inches (the longest) to 6 inches. Generally the large specimens were made of granite, and would require great patience and great skill in cutting such a hard and tough stone to the required dimensions." (Mills, William C., *Ohio Archaeological Exhibit at the Jamestown Exposition*, 1909(?), p 47)

GLACIAL COPPER

Copper artifacts found in Ohio were not usually made from imported or traded-in material. Instead, glaciers carried much copper from the Isle Royale region and the northern shore of Lake Superior in a broad "footprint": "...the successive glacial periods distributed detached pieces of this metal, known as float or drift copper, over an area measuring... about six hundred miles north and south, and seven hundred miles east and west, with the Lake Superior copper region at its northern edge. (West, George A., *Copper: Its Mining and Use by the Aborigines of the Lake Superior Region*, 1929/1970, p 43)

CEREMONIAL PICKS

A rare and much-admired Ohio artifact is the so-called ceremonial pick from the Intrusive Mound people of the Late Woodland. The Dr. Gordon F. Meuser collection contained 13 fine examples, all from separate counties except two from Darke County. Interestingly, the two smallest examples (1 x 8 inches, Wyandot County; 1 x 6½ inches, Darke County) were both made of slate. The four granite specimens measured 1¼ x 12 inches, 1¼ x 10½ inches, 1¼ x 9½ inches, and, 1¼ x 8¾ inches. Average length of the granite picks, though width remained constant, was 10⅕ inches. The remaining seven picks were made of diorite and widths ranged from 1 to 1¼ inches. Lengths of the diorite picks was 9½, 10½, 12¼, 12½, 13, 14 and 14½ inches. The average length of the diorite specimens was 12⅓ inches. (*Indian Relic Collection – Estate of Dr. Gordon F. Meuser of Columbus, Ohio,* Garth's Auction Barn, Inc.)

LARGE BOATSTONE

One of Ohio's largest boatstones came from a mound near McConnellsville, Morgan County. Measuring 7 inches long, it had the typical two perforations. (Editorial Staff, "Recent Discoveries," *The Antiquarian,* Vol. 1 Part 1, January 1897, p 27)

ANTLER HARPOONS

A number of antler harpoons were recovered from the Madisonville site, Hamilton County, a Mississippian-era village. The harpoons were about 6 to 10 inches long and had a single barb near the pointed tip. A hole was drilled near the base for line attachment, and most bases were irregular and not as well finished as the remainder of the pieces. (Hooton, Earnest A., *Indian Village Site and Cemetery Near Madisonville, Ohio,* 1920, p 58 plate 11)

FLINTRIDGE MATERIAL

Flint from Flintridge, the official gemstone of Ohio, has

fascinated humans in the state since earliest prehistoric times. The quarries of southeastern Licking County are best known for rainbow-colored flints, but there were many other varieties from which artifacts were chipped. Following are some of them: Blue or grey-blue translucent; glassy, from near-transparent to opaque; dark red through yellow shades; banded or ribbon with stripes of black, brown or grey; chalcedony in hues of blue, brown, green, purple, red, white and yellow; deep red and yellow with touches of lilac; lilac with quartz crystals; yellow with chalcedony and quartz crystals; brecciated (mentioned elsewhere); solid yellow; red and yellow; grey with red and yellow; leek-green; grey with purple, red and yellow; light grey mottled with grey and brown. (Mills, William C., "Flint Ridge," *Ohio Archaeological & Historical Society Publications*, Vol. XXX, 1921, pp 109-126)

ARTIFACT ILLUSTRATIONS

For amateur and professional archaeologists of yesteryear, sketches, drawings and photographs were available in the late 1800s. "Authors and Collectors / Desiring illustrations / of collections or archaeological subjects, should correspond with / The Harper Illustrating Synd. / Columbus, Ohio." (Advertisement, *The Antiquarian*, Vol. 1 Part 1, January 1897, p 28)

PASSENGER PIGEONS

Given the huge numbers of wild or passenger pigeons reported in early historic accounts—areas were even named after the birds, such as Pigeon Roost Swamp, northern Fairfield County—it is puzzling that few bones of these birds are found in prehistoric village middens. Either the pigeons were not in Ohio at certain times or they existed in smaller numbers or were not a major food resource. (Hothem, Lar, various sources)

MOUNDS IN COUNTIES

Some Ohio counties in the early part of this century had

many more mounds than others. Examples: Ross, 370; Licking, 225; Butler, 221; Jackson and Pickaway, each 173. (Mills, William C., *Archeological Atlas of Ohio*, 1914, p III)

MUSICAL ARTIFACTS

Very little is known about sound-making devices in ancient Ohio, and since many instruments may have been made of wood the evidence has largely disappeared due to the action of bacteria. A few musical devices known to have been used are: Copper rattles (Hopewell); bone rasps (deer and elk ribs), rattles and whistles, bird-skull (turkey) rattles (Ft. Ancient); turtle-shell rattles (Ft. Ancient); copper turtle-shell replica rattles, small-size (Hopewell); bone whistles and flutes from the hollow bones of large birds (Ft. Ancient). (Osburn, Mary H., "Prehistoric Musical Instruments in Ohio," *Ohio Archaeological & Historical Society Publications*, Vol. LV, 1946, pp 12-20)

SERPENT MOUND FINDS

Long ago Ohio's Serpent Mound was recognized as being unique, so also supposedly any artifacts found in the vicinity. "Relics From the Famous Serpent Mound. ...As I have lived within a few miles of this structure for a long while I have gathered an interesting collection of specimens from near it. These are very valuable because of their association with the famous Serpent. I will sell my collection for $25. I will mail anyone sending me $2 a stone hatchet, some arrow-heads, beads, and a few other relics found near the Serpent before it was made into a park. I will mail a fine arrow-head, to any address, for 24 cents in stamps. Correspondence desired with those who wish to purchase relics. As my collection has cost me much money and time I will not exchange. I sell for cash only. Write for description of what I have. WARREN COWEN, HIGHLAND Co., HILLSBORO, O." (Advertisement, *The Archaeologist*, Vol. 2 No. 3, March 1894, outside back cover)

GARTNER PIT CONTENTS

At the Gartner Village site along the Scioto River in Ross County, partially excavated in 1903, numerous large pits were found. Over one hundred of these Ft. Ancient pits were explored, and about 20% were discovered to be storage bins. These contained charred corn, beans, hickory nuts, butternuts, hazelnuts, chestnuts, and walnuts, plus pawpaw and wild plum seeds. The charred condition was possibly due to accidental fire. The remainder of the pits had been emptied of storage food and were used to dump household trash. Evidence suggests the bins were depleted in winter and refilled with debris in a general warm-weather house-cleaning. (Mills, William C., "Explorations of the Gartner Mound and Village Site," *Ohio Archaeological & Historical Society Publications*, Vol. XIII, 1904, pp 149-152, 156)

COPPER MOUND ARTIFACTS

The largest number of copper tools (technically, tool parts) ever found in an Ohio mound came from Hopewell Mound No. 25 in Ross County. The mound complex was excavated in 1891-92 by Warren K. Moorehead. Artifacts from No. 25, the primary mound, included 66 copper celt and adz heads. Individual weights were from 4 ounces to 38 pounds. (Hothem, Lar, *Treasures of the Mound Builders*, 1989, p 90)

BELLSON ADVERTISEMENT

Over half a century ago, in the depths of the financial paralysis known as the Great Depression, collecting activity in Ohio still continued. "PREHISTORIC INDIAN RELICS / ...Fine steatite paint cup, 1¼ x 1¼ inches, deeply cupped, Ohio. $1.25. ...Nice assorted arrowheads from Ohio, 15 for $1.00. ...Bellson Company, Box 229, Marion, Ohio" (Advertisement, *North American Indian Relic Collectors Association / Official Bulletin*, Vol. 1 No. 2, February 1935, p 12)

1 — Lanceolate point or knife, Late Paleo period, 3¾ inches long. Ex-collection Brison, this example is made of blue Upper Mercer flint and was found in Licking County. Larry Garvin, **Back to Earth***, Ohio*

2 — Paleo point or blade, lightly fluted, 3⅜ inches long. Material is pale grey Upper Mercer. This Dalton-like artifact is from Delaware County. Fred Winegardner collection, Ohio

*3 — Lanceolate, Late Paleo period, 3½ inches long. It is made from dark blue Upper Mercer flint. This piece is from Hardin County. Larry Garvin, **Back to Earth**, Ohio*

*4 — Paleo knife, 3⅜ inches long. It is made of grey and black Upper Mercer flint with lightning lines. The knife is from Muskingum County. Larry Garvin, **Back to Earth**, Ohio*

5 — Late Paleo stemmed lance with basal graver spur, 2⅝ inches long. Ex-collection Loughman, this was chipped from blue Upper Mercer flint and is from Licking County. Fred Winegardner collection, Ohio

*6 — Knife, probably Paleo period, in black Upper Mercer flint with several quartz lightning lines. It measures 3⅜ inches long and is from Muskingum County. Larry Garvin, **Back to Earth**, Ohio*

27

7 — *Late Paleo lance or knife, grey Upper Mercer flint, 3³⁄₈ inches long. This piece was a personal find of the owner in Licking County. Fred Winegardner collection, Ohio*

8 — *Dovetail or St. Charles blade, Early Archaic period, 3³⁄₈ inches long. It is chipped in blue and tan Upper Mercer flint that has touches of orange. Ex-collection McDaniel, it has the classic lenticular cross-section. Shelby County. Larry Garvin, **Back to Earth**, Ohio*

*9 — Newton Falls, Early Archaic point or blade, made of mottled blue Upper Mercer flint from eastern Ohio. Very symmetrical, it was found in Coshocton County. Larry Garvin, **Back to Earth**, Ohio*

10 — Early Archaic beveled blade, done in dark Upper Mercer flint, 2¼ inches long. This piece is of interest in that it has been extensively resharpened, making the blade quite narrow and sharply beveled. Muskingum County. Fred Winegardner collection, Ohio

11 — Early Archaic bifurcated knife form, 1¼ x 2¾ inches. Made of milky and blue Flintridge, this blade has a rounded tip and heavily serrated sides. It was picked up by the owner's grandfather, Frederick Davis, in 1962 while surface-hunting in Licking County. Scott Haskins collection, Ohio

12 — Early Archaic blade, 1⅜ x 3 inches long. Material is translucent blue-grey Flintridge with both darker and lighter inclusions. Ex-collection Olenick, Licking County. Scott Haskins collection, Ohio

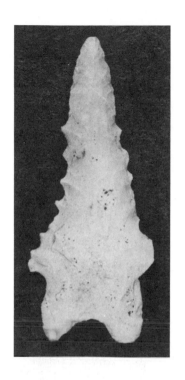

13 — Bifurcated blade, Early Archaic, made of greyish-tan Delaware (County) flint. The serrations are worn down on one edge. It is 2¾ inches long and from Perry County. Fred Winegardner collection, Ohio

14 — Bifurcated blade, Early Archaic, 1⅜ x 2⅛ inches. This is a thin piece in light tan and blue Upper Mercer with mottled and streaked colors. Ohio, county unknown. Scott Haskins collection, Ohio

15 — *Bifurcated blade, Early Archaic, 2⅛ inches. With nicely balanced base, the blue Upper Mercer artifact is from Coshocton County. Fred Winegardner collection, Ohio*

16 — *Bifurcated blade, Early Archaic, 1⅝ x 3⅛ inches. This is an exceptionally large and fine example in jewel material, cream and purple Flintridge. Ex-collection Joe Redick, Licking County. Scott Haskins collection, Ohio*

17 — Bifurcated Early Archaic blades. Left, 1¼ inches, translucent brownish unknown flint, Fairfield County. Right, 1½ inches, blue-black Upper Mercer flint, Licking County. Lar Hothem collection, Ohio

18—Bifurcated Early Archaic blades. Left, 1⅞ inches, medium-blue Upper Mercer, from McKean, Ohio. Right, 1⅞ inches, dark blue Upper Mercer, Franklin County. Lar Hothem collection, Ohio

33

19 — Bifurcated blade, Early Archaic, 1³/₁₆ x 1¹³/₁₆ inches. This delicate and beautifully chipped example is made of amber jewel Flintridge. Ex-collection Gary Davis, Paint Creek area, Ross County. Scott Haskins collection, Ohio

20 — Notched-base blade, Early Archaic period, 3 inches long. It is made of dark blue Upper Mercer. Excurvate edges indicate little resharpening for this example. Coshocton County. Larry Garvin, **Back to Earth**, *Ohio*

21 — Bifurcated blade, Early Archaic period, 1⅝ inches. Material is grey and black Upper Mercer, ex-collection Champion. Knox County. Fred Winegardner collection, Ohio

22 — Archaic notched-base blade, blue Upper Mercer flint, 3¾ inches long. This is a very symmetrical and well-made example in high-grade mottled flint. Ohio, county unknown. Fred Winegardner collection, Ohio

23 — Archaic notched-base blade, 2³⁄₄ inches long. It is made of blue and grey Upper Mercer flint and is from Ohio, county unknown. Fred Winegardner collection, Ohio

24 — Unnotched notched-base, Early Archaic, 1⁷⁄₈ x 3¹⁄₈ inches. Ex-collection Butler, it is pale blue Upper Mercer, from Perry County. Fred Winegardner collection, Ohio

25 — Early Archaic beveled blade, 1⅝ x 2⅝ inches. This deep-notch example is made of translucent jewel Flintridge in three colors. Licking County. Lar Hothem collection, Ohio

26 — Unnotched notched-base, Early Archaic period, 3¾ inches long. This fine large blade is chipped in dark blue Upper Mercer and is from Ohio, county unknown. Fred Winegardner collection, Ohio

27 — *Stemmed Kirk blade, Archaic, 2⅛ inches long. This piece, in mottled Upper Mercer flint, is ex-collection Loughman and from Licking County. Fred Winegardner collection, Ohio*

28 — *Short-stemmed Archaic blade, serrated, 2½ inches long. The interesting knife form is made of milky high-grade Flintridge and came from Licking County. Fred Winegardner collection, Ohio*

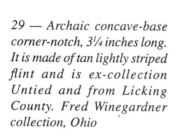

29 — Archaic concave-base corner-notch, 3¼ inches long. It is made of tan lightly striped flint and is ex-collection Untied and from Licking County. Fred Winegardner collection, Ohio

30 — Early Archaic beveled blade, 3¼ inches long. This slightly resharpened example is ex-collection Atkinson and is from Ohio, county unknown. Fred Winegardner collection, Ohio

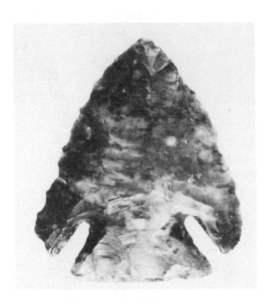

31 — Archaic diagonal-notch blade, 2⅛ inches long. Ex-collection Shipley, this piece is made of quality Upper Mercer and is from Delaware County. Fred Winegardner collection, Ohio

32 — Early Archaic blades, both Ohio. Left, 1¹³/₁₆ inches, butterscotch and blue Flintridge, county unknown. Right, 1⅞ inches, pink and purple Flintridge, ex-collection Billy Hillen, Fayette County. Scott Haskins collection, Ohio

33 — Heavy-duty serrated blade, 1 x 2⁷/₁₆ inches. Material is dark blue Upper Mercer and the artifact is from Licking County. Lar Hothem collection, Ohio

34 — Drill, Archaic period, 2⅛ inches long. It is chipped in Upper Mercer with a single lightning line and is from near Nevada, Wyandot County. Scott Haskins collection, Ohio

35 — Concave-base corner-notch, Archaic, 1½ x 2⅝ inches. This blade is made of multicolor Flintridge and is Ohio, county unknown. Scott Haskins collection, Ohio

*36 — Side-notch Archaic point or blade, 2¼ inches long. Material is jewel translucent lavender Flintridge and the piece is from Knox County. Larry Garvin, **Back to Earth**, Ohio*

37 — Pentagonal point or blade, Archaic, 2 inches long. It is made of striated Flintridge with brick red upper blade and tip. This was obtained at a Max Shipley auction and is from Licking County. Fred Winegardner collection, Ohio

38 — Knife, probably Woodland period, 5½ inches long. This large and well-chipped blade is made of dark Upper Mercer and was found in Logan County. Fred Winegardner collection, Ohio

39 — Stemmed blade, Adena and Early Woodland period, 3¼ inches long. Material is light-colored quality Flintridge and the piece was found in Wood County. Larry Garvin, Back to Earth, Ohio

40 — Adena stemmed blade, Early Woodland, 1⅞ x 4⅜ inches. It was chipped in mixed jewel Flintridge in white, cream and grey and came from Richland County. Lar Hothem collection, Ohio

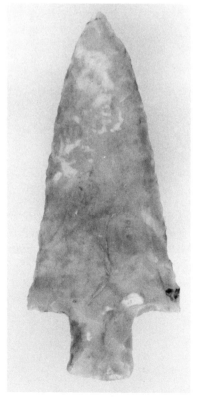

41 — Stemmed Adena blade, Early Woodland, $1^{15}/_{16}$ x $3^{3}/_{8}$ inches. Material is creamy-tan Flintridge with blue-grey inclusions. Ex-collection Myers Campbell, Delaware County. Scott Haskins collection, Ohio

42 — Adena stemmed blade, Early Woodland, $1^{1}/_{2}$ x $2^{11}/_{16}$ inches. Material is unusual, being multicolor Flintridge that has become deeply stained after being submerged in water. Marion County. Scott Haskins collection, Ohio

*43 — Middle Woodland point or blade, Hopewell, 3¼ inches long. In reddish mottled Flintridge, this artifact was found in Hardin County. Larry Garvin, **Back to Earth**, Ohio*

44 — Hopewell blade, Middle Woodland period, 3½ inches long. Ex-collections Helman, Kley and Merkel, this piece in translucent jewel Flintridge is from Darke County. Fred Winegardner collection, Ohio

45 — *Jacks Reef point, Late Woodland period, 1¹⁵⁄₁₆ inches long. This Intrusive Mound artifact is made of blue Upper Mercer with a lightning line, and is from Wyandot County. Scott Haskins collection, Ohio*

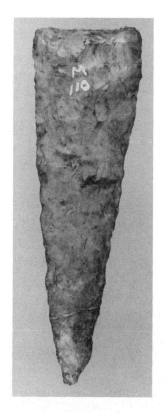

46 — *Ft. Ancient triangular knife, Mississippian, 4¹⁄₄ inches long. Material is cream and grey Upper Mercer. Ex-collection Hawks, it is from Ohio, county unknown. Fred Winegardner collection, Ohio*

47 — Ft. Ancient triangular knife, Mississippian, 4½ inches long. The greyish flint is probably Upper Mercer, and the piece has the diagnostic squared baseline. It came from Ross County. Fred Winegardner collection, Ohio

48 — Duo-tipped blade, Ft. Ancient, 5⅛ inches long. This knife is ex-collection Pinkston and is made of brownish Delaware County flint. Ohio, county unknown. Fred Winegardner collection, Ohio

ROCK-SHELTER IMAGE

A petroglyph of a deer-like animal was reported in 1947 by Robert Goslin near Kettle Hill rock-shelter in Fairfield County. The outline figure is approximately 12½ inches in length and 10 inches high. (Swauger, James L., *Petroglyphs of Ohio*, 1984, pp 274-275)

OHIO PICTOGRAPH

As compared to the petroglyphs (pecked or scratched images), Ohio may once have had a genuine pictograph (painted image). "The noted 'Narrows of Licking' are in the eastern part of the county. This is a very picturesque spot; cliffs of sandstone rock, fifty feet in height, line the sides of the canal, especially on the left bank of the stream. In some places they hang over in semicircular form, the upper portion projecting and defending the lower from the rains and weather. In one of those spots the aborigines chose to display their ingenuity at pictorial writing by figuring on the smooth face of the cliff, at an elevation of eight or ten feet above the water, the outlines of wild animals, and among the rest the figure of a huge black human hand. From this circumstance the spot is known to all the old hunters and inhabitants of this vicinity by the name of 'the black hand narrows.' In quarrying for the Ohio Canal the black hand was destroyed." (Howe, Henry, *Historical Collections of Ohio*, Vol. II, 1896, p 93)

KNIFE RIVER MATERIAL

Knife River flint was occasionally used for Early Paleo fluted points and later Hopewell (Middle Woodland) chipped artifacts. It is a fairly distinctive material, being dark honey colored and with whitish cloud-like inclusions. However, another flint (and discounting a somewhat similar Flintridge variety) may sometimes be confused with Knife River. "The lamellar blade or flake knife was made from a mottled, translucent brownish chalcedony which many archaeologists in the

Midwest would call Knife River flint from North Dakota. ...this flint type is found in some quantity in the northern part of the Lake Superior Basin. This raises the question as to the origin of similar flint which has been found in Hopewell sites in Wisconsin, Illinois, and Ohio." (Griffin, James Bennett and George Irving Quimby, "The McCollum Site," *Lake Superior Copper and the Indians: Miscellaneous Studies of Great Lakes Prehistory*, 1961, p 98)

PEARLS IN MOUNDS

Huge numbers of pearls were once placed in certain Ohio mounds, especially those of the Hopewell people. Guesses have been made about the value these organic gems once had, before they were ruined by long-term contact with the earth. "Immense quantities of these beautiful objects have been discovered in the ancient mounds erected by a forgotten race in the Mississippi valley, especially in certain points in Ohio. ...From a mound in the Little Miami valley, Professor F. W. Putnam obtained over 60,000 pearls, nearly two bushels, drilled and undrilled. Two other deposits yielded upward of 100,000 pearls." ("Notes," *The American Archaeologist*, Vol. 2 Part 11, November 1898, pp 305-306)

CANADIAN BANNERSTONES

Ontario, due north of Ohio and Canada's closest province to the state, has a number of bannerstone types also found in Ohio. These include: Curved pick, winged and "butterfly" winged, panel, double-bitted axe, tubular, fluted ball, and geniculate. (*Annual Report for 1929*, National Museum of Canada, Bull. 67, 1931, p 108 and plate IX)

PREHISTORIC TERRACES

The lower portion of Caesar's Creek in Warren County may be the site of unusual earthworks, possibly made for prehistoric agriculture or habitation or both. "As to the terraces themselves they are to be found on both sides of the creek. They are found from a point about half a mile down the creek from the new iron bridge on the Waynesville and Clarkesville road, nearly or quite to the point where the valley of Caesar's Creek enters that of the Miami. They are not continuous or unbroken; they end abruptly a little before reaching a ravine, then start the same way a little beyond; then there may be a wide interval between one terrace or group of terraces and another. There may be but a single terrace on the hillside, or there may be two, three or even four, one above the other. They run quite horizontally along the hillside, the general width is about a rod (16½ feet), but some of them are thirty or forty feet in width. ...One of the most interesting groups is on Mr. Hisey's farm. The whole hillside is wrought out into broad platforms, the upper one being the broadest and shortest, the face of the hill behind, having been dug away so as to form an amphitheatre with an arc of about 180 yards. ...As a general thing the terraces, when in groups, are from 200 to 300 yards in length. Some single ones are much longer. ...The aggregate length of those which have been discovered and traced along Caesar's Creek is more than 5850 yards, or considerably exceeding three miles." (Brown, Thomas J., "Prehistoric Artificial Terraces in Ohio," *The American Antiquarian*, May 1888, Vol. X No. 3, pp 168-170)

VALENTINE CACHE

The Valentine cache was discovered in Lake County, Ohio, in 1978. A total of 103 complete or partial blades was recovered, plus 41 fragments. The material was Flintridge in various colors and with crystalline inclusions. There were four basic blade shapes, including tear-drop, leaf, nearly parallel-sided, and convex-sided. Length range for all specimens was from about 2¾ to 5⅜ inches. (Bush, David R., "The Valentine Cache Site / Lake County, Ohio," *Ohio Archaeologist*, Vol. 29 No. 1, Winter 1979, pp 21-24)

ARCHAEOLOGICAL LECTURES

There was a time when persons desiring archaeological information had no readily available means of mass communication. Instead, public speakers presented the latest, authoritative reports. "Interesting Illustrated Lectures—Upon—THE CLIFF DWELLER, THE MOUND BUILDER, THE AMERICAN INDIAN. By Warren K. Moorehead. The stereoptican views are numerous and very fine. They illustrate the Hopewell Group, Ft. Ancient, the Cliff Dwellings, great ruins and fortifications, relics, etc. ...In Cincinnati, St. Louis, Chicago, Columbus, Cleveland and other cities were these lectures heard by large audiences and favorably reviewed by the press. ...For churches, schools, Y.M.C.A.'s and general lecture courses they are just what is wanted. For terms write to SHEARER'S LECTURE BUREAU, 9th and Walnut Streets, Cincinnati, Ohio." (Advertisement, *The Archaeologist*, Vol. 3 No. 7, July 1895, inside front cover)

COLLECTING AND CONSERVATION

Collectors of prehistoric North American artifacts do a positive thing in acquiring and protecting cultural objects from the distant past. This process was well described by one of this state's foremost collector-archaeologists: "...We, as collectors of Indian artifacts, are conservationists at heart and must feel the need for trying to keep at least a part of this great country in the clean untainted state that existed during the days of Indian ownership. Let's help preserve the remnants of the Indians and the America they knew and loved." (Vietzen, Raymond C., "From the Council Lodge," *Ohio Indian Relic Collectors Society*, Bulletin No. 21, January 1949)

WACHTEL ARTIFACTS

Extra-fine Ohio artifacts once in the Hubert Wachtel collection included: Winged single-notch banner, 4⅛ x 7¾ inches, Montgomery County; bar amulet of red slate with flared ends,

9 inches, Erie County; curved-pick banner of slate, largest known at 10 inches, provenance Ohio; flint crescent blade 5⅝ inches long or wide, Preble County; Dovetail Flintridge drill 3 inches long, Licking County; Hopewell notched blade with quartz inclusion, 4⅜ inches, Medina County; Dovetail, colorful small-base type, 4½ inches, Perry County; Dovetail, multicolor Flintridge, 5⁵⁄₁₆ inches, Franklin County; Dovetail, translucent Flintridge, 5¼ inches, Auglaize County. (Lamb, E. Wendell and Josephine and Lawrence W. Shultz, *More Indian Lore*, 1968, pp 172-179)

TROPHY AXES

Only about 20 classic Ohio-type trophy axes have been found, these having true trophy characteristics. Such factors include very unusual and colorful materials (quartzite, gneiss), highly stylized forms, and heavy overall smoothing and polish. (Baldwin, John, "Ohio Trophy Axes," *The Redskin*, Vol. XIII No. 3, 1978, p 94)

ZALESKI PALEO POINT

An exceptional Paleo point was found in Ross County in the early 1900s, with both faces fluted nearly to the tip. One of the larger complete Cumberland-type artifacts from Ohio, it was made of black Zaleski flint. Length was 3¹¹⁄₁₆ inches. (Bailey, Howard F., "An Outstanding Cumberland Point," *Ohio Archaeologist*, Vol. 32 No. 3, Summer 1982, p 16)

COLLECTOR/ARCHAEOLOGISTS

Those interested in prehistoric artifacts a century ago were not necessarily only collectors; some were more amateur archaeologists. "Flint implements to exchange for photographs and drawings of Indians and relics and archaeological maps. F. E. Bingman, Box 162, Jackson, Ohio." ("Exchange Department," *The Archaeologist*, Vol. 3 No. 7, July 1895, p 253)

OHIO GLACIAL MATERIAL

Some research has been done as to the locations in North America of raw materials from which prehistoric artifacts were made. Possibly some of the material arrived in Ohio by glacial action. The Canadian province of Ontario, to the north, contains various quantities of the following materials: Copper, diorite, soapstone, graphite, chert, chalcedony, hematite, quartz, mica, micaceous schist, granite and gneiss. (Laidlaw, Col. G. E., "Some Archaeological Notes on Victoria County, Ontario," *The Archaeological Bulletin*, May-June 1915, pp 52-54)

OHIO BANNERSTONE TYPES

A large number of bannerstones have been found in Ohio, recovered on a regular, if sparse, basis. The types include: Humped, Concave humped, Triangular (Type No. 4), Saddle-face (Type No. 7), Hinge (Type No. 9), Reel (Type No. 10), Double-bitted axe (Type No. 11), Geniculate (Type No. 13), Paneled (Type No. 14), Quartz butterfly (Type No. 20), Knobbed lunate (Type No. 22), Curved pick (Type No. 23), Single-pronged pick (Type No. 24), Double-notched butterfly (Type No. 25), Undrilled butterfly (Type No. 26), Notched ovate (Type No. 27), Double crescent (Type No. 28), Fluted ball (Type No. 30), Tubular (Type No. 31), and, Tubular-faced (Type No. 32). (Knoblock, Byron W., *Bannerstones of the North American Indian*, 1939, pp 159-170)

OHIO COLLECTING TRIPS

Early artifact collectors in Ohio often made trips or collecting expeditions within the state, talking with farmers who might have found specimens. At times unusual use was made of artifacts. One incident from such an excursion is included here. "Next man had no flints on hand, but had often picked them up to break for use in his old flint lock shot gun. 'I tell you,' said he, 'Them old flints have good fire in them.'" (Davis, J. H.,

"Some Notes on a Collecting Trip," *The Archaeologist*, Vol. 3 No. 4, April 1895, p 144)

PENDANT GENERALITIES

In general, Adena pendants are thick and well-made, while Hopewell pendants tend to be thin and well-made. Pendants from earlier Archaic times and the later Mississippian period seem to be more nondescript. (Hothem, Lar, various sources)

COLLECTOR ADVERTISEMENT

Even a century ago there were collectors and dealers active in the state. "SLATE, STONE AND FLINT IMPLEMENTS / Of all kinds, collected from central Ohio. Everything perfect. 3000 specimens. Write to / Z.Y. Corey / York, Union Co., O." (*The Archaeologist*, November 1893, p 229)

OHIO BLACK FLINT

Ohio has long been noted for having high-quality artifacts made of black flint. "In this competent and authoritative work (Stout, Wilber and R. A. Schoenlaub, *The Occurrence of Flint in Ohio*) is specifically mentioned a jet black flint as occurring in the abundant quarry sites (Upper Mercer) and workshops of Perry County. ...the black flint of Flint Ridge is usually attributed to its north-western marginal area. Black flint, with chalcedony structure, and particularly with quartz crypts or inclusions, strongly suggests Flint Ridge origin. ...Also a high grade flint in quarry and workshop sites of the Zaleski flint member in Vinton County is just as good and just as black as that from the Upper Mercer locations. (Kramer, Dr. Leon, "Is There a Jet Black Flint...," *Ohio Archaeologist*, Vol. 17 No. 2, April 1967, p 84)

WAYNE COUNTY FLUTED POINT

A fine fluted point made of tan flint was once picked up in

Wayne County, Ohio. The size of this outstanding specimen was 1⅛ x 5 inches. (Vietzen, Raymond C., *Yesterday's Ohioans*, 1973, p 66)

OHIO CENTENNIAL EXHIBIT

The state of Ohio had a large exhibit of prehistoric artifacts at the 1876 Centennial Exposition at Philadelphia; this was reported by Col. Charles Whittlesey, pioneer Ohio archaeologist after whom the Whittlesey Focus of northern Ohio was named. This Ohio display must have been impressive: "Although, from want of time, the Ohio collection could not be made complete, it stood next that of the Smithsonian in interest and value." The Ohio display included 189 grooved axes, shuttle-forms (gorgets) 45, circular stones (discoidals) 36, pipes 59, crescents 27, tubes 21, breastplates 3, perforated spheres (ball bannerstones) 27, pendants 73, boatstones 10, hemispheres (cones) 17, birdstones 9, slate bannerstones "highly polished and elegant" 30. There were many other more common artifacts at the Exposition as well. (Ohio State Board of Managers, *Ohio Centennial Report*, 1877, pp 5, 82, 85-87)

GLACIAL KAME PENDANT

Large and complete Glacial Kame gorgets or pendants are scarce in the state, but a fine example was found in northwestern Ohio. "The cannal [modern spelling, 'cannel'] coal pendant... was found in 1889, embedded in a silt deposit about six feet below surface, in an excavation for the C. & E. R'y bridge abutment, east bank of Auglaize River, Allen County, Ohio. This specimen is eight inches long by two inches in width and one-half inch in thickness; a jet black, polished, much worn, shows considerable use, and has three perforations — two near the small end and one just below the middle, on the face between the two upper holes, which are one-half inch apart; it is much worn to a perceptible depth, evidencing a suspension. There are 438 notches discernable [sic] on the corners and edges, which show quite plainly." (Pillars, James, "Letters to the Editor," *The Archaeologist*, Vol. 3 No. 4, April 1895, p 146)

HARDSTONE PENDANTS

Regarding hardstone, not slate, pendants and gorgets: "...of all the hardstone pendants I have handled in the past I was never aware of the tally marking on the edge of the smaller end. They are usually very faint, hardly discernible to the naked eye, but they can be felt with the fingernail and seen under a magnifying glass. After hearing this, I tested some and found it to be true in a lot or rather majority of cases." (Wachtel, Hubert C., "The Hardstones," *Ohio Archaeologist*, Vol. 17 No. 4, October 1967, p 155)

OHIO BLACK SLATE

The material source or origin for the slate in some Ohio artifacts may be within the state. "The Ohio black shale is the lowest stratum exposed in (Scioto) county. It outcrops along the west bank of the Scioto River. In color it is very black, is fine-grained, high in carbon, and crumbles after long exposure. The shale was used by prehistoric races in making gorgets and other ornaments." In Tremper Mound [Hopewell] "Ohio black shale was found in pieces of a size suggesting their use in the making of ornaments." (Galbreath, Charles B., *History of Ohio*, Vol. I, 1925, pp 45, 49)

OLD COLLECTION PERCENTAGES

What constituted a typical artifact collection a century ago is still a matter of interest today. "The percentage of specimens in the average collection is: Broken pottery, 21%; flint implements, 60%; axes, 4%; ungrooved axes (celts), 5%; whole pottery, spades, hoes, 2%; pestles and hammers, etc., 4%; hematites and ceremonials, 1%; pipes, ornaments, odd species, 3%." (Moorehead, Warren K., "Information for Collectors," *The Archaeologist*, Vol. 2 No. 10, October 1894, p 314)

PLUMMET THEORIES

A possible use for plummets was explained by the noted collector, Edward W. Payne: "Another interesting specimen, often found in mounds, is the so-called 'plummet' or 'sinker,' which closely resembles a plumb bob or net weight. We are of the opinion that the early people of North America, like the Chinese, Japanese, and Eskimo, did not have pockets in their clothing, but carried bags, or pouches, in which they kept their tools, pipes, ornaments, needles, thread, etc. These 'sinkers' were probably fastened to the end of the draw string which closed the pouch, then passed up under the belt or sash and allowed to drop down on the side of the belt, thus acting as a counter balance weight, which not only prevented the loss of the pouch but permitted its quick and easy removal." (Payne, Edward W., *The Immortal Stone Age*, 1938, p 34)

NORTHERN OHIO AXES

Regarding the frequency of hardstone axe or axe-like tool finds in northern Ohio: "...the number of axes found is far less than the celts even on sites where both are found. Many axes are found, at some distance from the villages, in the forests and on hillsides where prehistoric woodcutters left them." (Vietzen, Raymond C., *Indians of the Lake Erie Basin*, 1965, p 298)

JADE PENDANT

Very little jade has ever been picked up in Ohio. Over a century ago, however, a small polished pendant of jade was found in Miami County. (Fowke, Gerard, "Correspondence," *The Archaeologist*, Vol. 2 No. 2, February 1894, p 60)

MOUND PEARL DEPOSITS

Large deposits of freshwater pearls have been found in Ohio Hopewell mounds. These were used as decorative embellishments, some drilled as beads and buttons and others left plain. At the Hopewell Group, Moorehead found two caches. One contained about 16,000 pearls, the other about 19,000. Twenty-three pounds of pearls were found in Mound Three of the Turner Group. There were 36,000 pearls, with "several thousand" additional which had been largely destroyed by fire. (Willoughby, Charles C., *The Turner Group of Earthworks / Hamilton County, Ohio*, 1922, pp 52-53, Plate 11)

LITTLE-KNOWN EARTHWORKS

Some of the early archaeological reports in Ohio seem to refer to remains publicized at the time but about which little is known today. One such is: "Terraces on the Hills at Red Bank, near Pendleton (Hamilton County)." (Thomas, Cyrus, *Catalogue of Prehistoric Works East of the Rocky Mountains*, Bureau of American Ethnology, 1891, p 174)

OHIO ARCHAEOLOGICAL EDUCATION

Two Ohio centers of learning made exceptional advances in archaeology in the 1800s, as indicated by this account: "The oldest institution in the Central States which can lay claim to good work in archaeology is the Cincinnati Society of Natural History. Before any of the more progressive modern scientific institutions west of the Alleghanies [sic] were founded, it had published numerous reports and made a creditable and an intelligent collection. Its work dates from 1870. Along with it should be mentioned the Western Reserve Historical Society of Cleveland, which is much older and so far as history is concerned its work out-ranks any of the western institutions." (Moorehead, Warren K., "Archaeology in the Central States," *The Archaeologist*, Vol. 2 No. 2, February 1894, p 53)

BARNESVILLE PETROGLYPHS

There are not many Ohio petroglyphs that can be seen today, but one group in the southeastern part of the state is justly famous: "Among the most interesting relics of the mound-building race are the 'Barnesville track rocks' on the sand rock of the coal measure located on the lands of Robert G. Price. They were discovered in 1856 by a son of Mr. Price. The tracks are those of birds', animals', and human feet, and other figures, as shellfish, serpents, earthworms, circles, stars, etc.: These indentations vary from two to over twenty inches in length. The depths of the impressions are from three-fourths of an inch to a scale hardly perceptible." (Howe, Henry, *Historical Collections of Ohio*, Vol. I, 1896, p 325)

COLLECTOR'S LAMENT

A heartfelt collector's complaint and two questionable remedies come down to us from across the years: "Of course these interesting objects [a flint knife and a copper bracelet] fell into the hands of a person whose interest in such things is only as deep as the monetary value he places on them, and I have found that the more ignorant such a person is archaeologically, the more valuable he thinks any object which falls into his hands and a great many of the most important finds do happen to go to that class of people. ...This is one of the disappointments a true collector is bound to find out, and there seems to be no remedy unless we could pass a law authorizing confiscation by the state, or by hanging the individual." (Rayner, J. A., "Notes From the Miami Valley," *The Archaeological Bulletin*, Vol. 5 No. 3, May-June 1914, p 36)

OHIO ARCHAEOLOGICAL CONVENTION

An 1875 convention was held in Mansfield, Ohio, to bring together people and artifacts in order to form a state association. The founding purpose was as follows: "The undersigned, aware of the facts that Ohio presents one of the richest fields for the study of Archaeology, as embraced especially in the relics of a race anterior and more cultivated than that found here during the eighteenth and nineteenth centuries; that while in almost every county there are one or more persons who have studied the subject and collected some relics, there has been no well organized system pursued, and no combined effort made

60

to elicit the truth, and settle inquiring minds upon a well sustained theory of who they were, or when or how long they inhabited the country we now occupy. These relics are becoming yearly more interesting by discoveries of objects left by them, which have never been combined, and are being lost or destroyed." (*Minutes of the Ohio State Archaeological Convention*, 1875, p 3)

BAUM PLANT FOODS

The Fort Ancient site of Baum Village had storage pits with the remains of many different plant foods. These included corn of both six-row and eight-row varieties, kidney bean, three kinds of hickory nut, butternut, walnut, pawpaw, hazelnut, chestnut, wild red plum and wild grape. (Galbreath, Charles B., *History of Ohio*, Vol. I, 1925, pp 35-36)

HILLTOP ENCLOSURE WATER PROBLEM

Regarding Ohio's hill-top enclosures: "...the most perplexing question in the study of all these forts, one that has never been solved in a satisfying manner, is that of water supply. No springs exist within them, as they are above water drainage; shallow depressions in some have been called reservoirs, but these would be very precarious as they depend entirely upon rainfall and are dry much of the summer and autumn; it would be a tedious and arduous undertaking to carry an adequate supply up these long steep hills at any time, and with an active, alert enemy at hand would be impossible of performance. Even should the few ponds be cleared out to a depth that would ensure plenty of water the year round, the difficulty still presents itself that most of these enclosures have no depression within them where water would stand for a day." (Fowke, Gerard, *Archaeological History of Ohio*, 1902, p 238)

ADENA TABLET USE

Theories have been put forth that Adena formal tablets (with stylized designs on one face and several grooves on the back) were ceremonial or ritual body stamps. The design side may have made the marks, and tattooing instruments could have been shaped and pointed on the reverse. In support of this theory, one tablet was found with three pointed bone "awls," while traces of red ochre were found on both the Cincinnati (Hamilton County) and the Berlin (Jackson County) tablets. Interestingly, small pieces of rubbed and ground hematite are sometimes found in Adena mounds. (Hothem, Lar, various sources)

O.S.U. ARCHAEOLOGICAL STUDY

The official and institutionalized study of Archaeology in the state began at The Ohio State University just over a century ago, at Orton Hall. "The Trustees of this University have established this new department in the fire-proof Museum erected by the State of Ohio upon the University campus. The Curator of the Department [Warren K. Moorehead] desires that all Ohio collectors and collectors from other states interested in the preservation of antiquities, and having good and valuable collections for exchange, or portions of collections, correspond with him regarding the placing of such specimens as they have for exchange, or donation, in the Museum. The Museum offers a safe and permanent repository for all specimens donated to it." (Moorehead, Warren K., *The Archaeologist*, Vol. 2 No. 4, April 1894, back cover announcement)

LORAIN COUNTY CLOVIS POINT CACHE

Around 1900 a cache of fluted Early Paleo Clovis points was found in Lorain County, close to a creek. The artifacts were made of grey Onondaga (New York) flint and the 12 specimens were from 2½ to 3 inches long. (Vietzen, Raymond C., *Yesterday's Ohioans*, 1973, p 32)

FAR-FETCHED MOUND THEORY

Various authors in the 1800s put forth theories that mound-builders co-existed with the giant elephants known as mammoths and mastodons. Wesley Bradford, writing in *American Antiquities* (1841, p 226) and referenced in N. H. Winchell's *The Aborigines of Wisconsin* (1911, p 12) had this to say: "There is nothing improbable in the supposition that the mastodon was known to the mound builders." This idea was taken many steps along by writers who suggested that Ohio's Fort Ancient was such a stupendous accomplishment that mere humans could not have done the earth-moving unassisted. It was suggested that mastodons were harnessed to be huge draft animals and used for the construction of walls and mounds. We now know all this to be untrue. The fact is, however, that much earlier Paleo peoples were indeed familiar with giant elephants. Authors from the 1800s were right about the animal-human contact but were wrong about the time—they were off by about ten thousand years. (Hothem, Lar, various sources)

PORTAGE COUNTY BLADE CACHE

In 1982 a large cache of Adena blades was found in Portage County. Known as the Lukens cache, it contained 342 blades. Since seven blades were found both before and after the discovery of the main cache, it in fact consisted of 356 blades. The material was high-grade Flintridge. (Converse, Robert, "The Lukens Cache," *Ohio Archaeologist*, Vol. 34 No. 3, Summer 1984, pp 20, 27)

UNKNOWN SHAPING TOOL

A mystery tool of some sort seems to have been used to shape or finish some of the finest Ohio artifacts. This tool was used both in the Late Archaic (for birdstones) and the Middle Woodland (for Hopewell platform pipes). The marks, while much resembling the regular spacing of teeth on a modern metal file, have been found on a few old and authentic artifacts. The tool left narrow, shallow furrows that were nearly equidistant, about the same depth, and often about the same length. Due to the fact that the marks are found just beneath the surface polish, the tool may have been used more for final touches than for the actual shaping. No readily available natural material is known that can reproduce the regularity and uniformity of these markings. (Townsend, Earl C. Jr., *Birdstones of the North American Indian*, 1959, pp 235-240; McGuire, Joseph D., *Pipes and Smoking Customs of the American Aborigines*, Report of the U. S. National Museum, 1899, p 514)

NORTHERN OHIO CACHES

Caches, the finding of buried artifacts in groups, are always fascinating. "Many interesting caches of leaf-shaped blades consisting of large numbers were found throughout the lake basin. ...The largest and finest of these caches was found in 1887 or 1888 (at or near) Botzum, Summit County, Ohio in the Cuyahoga valley. Several nearby mounds appear to be Hopewellian. There were 103 thin, leaf-shaped blades of red, tan and gray mottled flint ridge material... Another cache of flint ridge leaf-shaped forms was found in the Huron River valley near Milan, Erie County, Ohio. There were 35 expertly worked thin blades of pink, red and white mottled flint from the Ridge. In size the blades were quite uniform averaging three to three and one-half inches in length by two inches in width." (Vietzen, Raymond C., *Indians of the Lake Erie Basin or Lost Nations*, 1965, pp 83-84)

COLLECTING ADVANTAGES

Some astute observations have been made about collecting, with probable application to old-time collections in Ohio. "The class of men who have the greatest opportunity to make collections at small expense are country physicians and storekeepers. In the doctor's travels throughout his county he meets many farmers who have a number of specimens and it is therefore not surprising that the largest percentage of collectors are physicians. The storekeepers often exchange goods with farmers and thus secure many hundred relics yearly." (Moorehead,

Warren K., "Information for Collectors," *The Archaeologist*, Vol. 2 No. 1, January 1894, p 28)

OHIO FLINT SOURCES

In addition to Ohio's major and well-known flint quarries, there were a number of other, smaller quarry sites: In the southcentral part of Jefferson Township, deposits of chalcedony, etc. (Coshocton County); between Walhonding and Warsaw, on the north side of the Mohican River (Coshocton County); "flint diggings" near Petrea (Jackson County); flint quarry three miles west of Brownsville (Licking County); "flint diggings" in the southwestern corner of county (Mahoning County); and, "flint diggings" at New Lexington (Perry County). (Thomas, Cyrus, *Catalogue of Prehistoric Works East of the Rocky Mountains*, Bureau of American Ethnology, 1891, pp 169, 175, 177, 179, 181)

AXES AND CELTS

In Ohio, as well as in most other Midwestern states, celts or ungrooved axes tend to be far more common field-finds than grooved axes. There are simply many more of them. This is so despite axes having been made for a longer period. In the Archaic, axes were made ca. 5000–1000 BC, for at least 4000 years, while celts were produced mainly ca. 1000 BC–AD 1600s, about 2600 years in Woodland and Mississippian times. One factor may be that the average celt is smaller than the average axe (hence easier to manufacture) so more were made. Of greater importance, though, is probable use and population. The Archaic is thought to have had a smaller number of people at earlier times, a population which increased from Early to Middle to Late in the period. Main axe use would have been for obtaining firewood, followed by various cutting and pounding tasks. The Woodland period had these same uses, plus a population that presumably increased into Mississippian times which began ca. AD 800. A novel use for celts then was agriculture, which required at least some clearing of forest. It is believed that neither axes nor celts actually were used to cut down trees. Instead, they were used to cut the bark (girdle) near the base, which quickly killed the trees, preventing leafing and shade. Trees were then either burned or crops were planted in a skeleton forest. (Hothem, Lar, various sources)

ISA—MIAMI BRANCH

There was an early artifact collector / amateur archaeological society called The International Society of Archaeologists, organized in 1909. Branch Society Number 3, in Ohio, was the Miami Branch, with officers Frank G. Burdett (Dayton), Charles Filbert (Miamisburg), and F. P. Thompson (Dayton). (*The Archaeological Bulletin*, Vol. 6 No. 3, May-June 1915)

STEATITE CONTAINER DISTRIBUTION

Steatite or soapstone containers, Late Archaic / Early Woodland, are quite scarce in Ohio, but fragments have been found. "There are… two areas in Ohio where steatite sherds occur; one in the northeast corner and the other in the southeastern portion of the state." (Gartley, Richard, "Distribution of Steatite Vessels in Ohio," *Ohio Archaeologist*, Vol. 26 No. 2, Spring 1976, pp 28-29)

COST OF MOOREHEADS'S BOOKS

Anyone interested in fine old archaeological books might also like to know the original prices of some. In particular, the publications written by Warren K. Moorehead will prove enlightening. *Primitive Man in Ohio*, 1892, sold for two dollars, as did *Fort Ancient*, 1890. *The Bird-Stone Ceremonial* cost fifty cents. (Moorehead, Warren K., *Prehistoric Implements*, 1900, back-of-book advertising pages)

MISSISSIPPIAN ANIMAL USE

The remains of mammals found at a late prehistoric site in northern Ohio provide a good sampling of what was hunted for food, furs/leather or bone material in that time and place. Species are listed in order of frequency found, followed by the number of bones recovered. Virginia deer (1160), raccoon (794), elk (324), beaver (304), black bear (285), gray squirrel (149), dog (95), porcupine (86), wildcat (47), otter (18), gray fox (12), mink (8), cottontail rabbit (8), chipmunk (7), woodchuck (6), muskrat (4), opossum (3), meadow mouse (3), cougar (1), and, fox squirrel (1). (Goslin, Robert, "Animal Remains," *The Fairport Harbor Village Site*, offprint from *Ohio State Archaeological & Historical Quarterly*, Vol. 52 No. 1, 1943, pp 43-45)

ARCHAEOLOGICAL NICKNAME

Ohio has long been termed the Buckeye State, but there was once another semi-official nickname which is rarely seen today. "[Mounds and earthworks] are scattered over 20 or more states, from the Mississippi River eastward to the Atlantic and extending southward to the Gulf and into Florida. Ohio, it may be truly said, was the center of Mound-builder life, as a result of which it has come to be known as the Mound-builder state." (Shetrone, H. C., *Primer of Ohio Archaeology -- The Mound Builders and the Indians*, 1951, p 6)

COLLECTING AND CHARACTER

Years ago an Ohio dealer (one with strong feelings about reading material) listed some reasons why artifact collecting was a positive, character-building activity.

"First: It induces young people to collect and preserve something.

Second: It creates a taste for reading literature that teems with the expression of wholesome thought.

Third: Careing [sic] for a collection creates a system of order.

Fourth: Elevating ideas.

Fifth: Betters the character of the individual.

Sixth: An enthusiastic collector has no need for trashy literature.

Seventh: Bad habits are well erased when a better one is substituted. The time given to collecting and the careing [sic] of a collection of curios curtails time sometime [sic] given to trashy novel reading and other frivolous allurements that are injurious."
(Nissley, J. R.,*Indian Relics / Illustrated Catalog No. 15*, Mansfield, Ohio, ca. 1930s, p 12)

SOUTHWESTERN OHIO FLINT

Materials used for Ohio chipped artifacts can be a complicated subject, but it is here somewhat clarified for the southwestern portion of Ohio. "Chipped flint, chert and other kinds of stone were found in abundance in both the Ft. Ancient and the Woodland village areas. The chipped objects were, for the most part, very crude, probably because of the inferior quality of the glacial and pebble flint that was available to the Indians. Flint is not native to the southwestern part of Ohio. Not only did the poor grade of raw material contribute to the inferior objects, but the fact that only small pebbles and boulders were available in the area prevented these people from attempting to make large, fine articles. True flint has a fine conchoidal fracture and when such material was obtainable, there is evidence of excellent workmanship in skillfully fashioned objects." (Oehler, Charles, "Flint," *Turpin Indians*, Cincinnati Museum of Natural History, 1973, p 12)

TOURING THROUGH TIME

The state of Ohio has long been attractive to those who study ancient remains. "Nothing could afford more pleasure than an automobile trip over the state of Ohio, and a view of the earthworks, found in nearly every part of that state, made by prehistoric men who no doubt thoroughly understood their business and the art of fortifying." (Payne, Edward W., *The Immortal Stone Age*, 1938, p 31)

OHIO ARCHAEOLOGICAL PUBLICATION

The Archaeologist, Ohio's pioneering archaeological magazine, was published in Columbus for three years, 1893 into 1895. It was issued monthly for each year except 1895, when the magazine terminated the Columbus connection with the September issue, Vol. 3 No. 9. This took place when it joined or was absorbed by *Popular Science News*, published in New York City, at 19 Liberty Street. *The Archaeologist*, of which individual copies are quite scarce, thus exists in 33 consecutive issues, 12 plus 12 plus 9. Anyone with a complete run has quite a paper treasure. (Moorehead, Warren K., *The Archaeologist*, Vol. 3 No. 9, September 1895, pp 321-322)

UNIQUE COLLECTIBLES

Worthy of thought (regarding prehistoric Ohio artifacts): "This 'Hobby' is entirely different from others. A stamp or coin is just as valuable to a collector whether accidentally procured or bought from a dealer. This is true because we already have the full history of the origin and life of people who made the stamp or coin, while the history of the former races of our country must be compiled principally from such artifacts as have been preserved from that far away time, and these same artifacts should never have been placed in the category of dollars and cents." (Rayner, J. A., *The Archaeological Bulletin*, March-April 1913, p 41)

VALUE OF VALUE

Also worthy of thought: Like all cultural art objects, value assigned (dollars and cents) is indeed one aspect of appreciation and definition and status. (Whether or not it is the prime consideration depends on the situation and individual.) The very fact that prehistoric North American artifacts have been and are worth money is simply a part of a free market economy, one that benefits most people much of the time and makes for a healthy, positive society. Because values are involved, and have been for at least 150 years, this has helped save countless millions of artifacts for study today. The artifacts have long been recognized and accepted as something worth holding onto and collecting, which is respect of the highest order. It would be a sad thing indeed if prehistoric artifacts were considered cultural trash and beneath notice or beyond caring. (Hothem, Lar, various sources)

OHIO ROCK INSCRIPTIONS

Col. Charles Whittlesey, one of Ohio's great early archaeologists, listed some of this state's scarce petroglyphs: "Localities of Inscribed Rocks...

2. One mile above Wellsville on the Ohio River, north shore, upon a flat surface of grit covered at high water — wrought in double channels by a pointed tool, like a pick...

4. Nearly opposite the mouth of 'Wheeling Creek,' below Wheeling City, on the north bank of the Ohio...

8. Near Burlington, Lawrence County, O., on the north side of the Ohio, 3 miles above...

9. Near Hanging Rock, on the River, Lawrence Co., Ohio.

10. A Colossal human head, on a flat rock, only visible at low water; a few miles above Portsmouth, Ohio.

11. 'Turkey foot Rock' — Maumee City, Lucas County, Ohio, on a block of limestone, at the foot of the rapids."

(Whittlesey, Charles, "Rock Inscriptions in the United States," *Western Reserve and Northern Ohio Historical Society*, No. 42, March 1878, pp 53-54)

LARGE ADENA BLADE

A superb large Ohio Adena blade was found in Mercer County in 1958. Made of mottled (blue to tan) Flintridge material, the artifact measured 2¾ x 6⅝ inches. (Editor, *The Redskin*, Vol. II No. 3, 1967, p 101)

EARLY CACHE REPORT

One of the earliest reports of a cache of Woodland blades is contained in a letter by a Dr. Hildreth, Marietta, dated 1819: "There was lately found at Waterford, not far from the bank of the Muskingum, a magazine of spear and arrow heads, sufficient to fill a peck measure. They laid in one body, occupying a space of about eight inches in width and 18 in length, and at one end about a foot from the surface of the earth, and 18 inches at the other; as though they had been buried in a box, and one end had sunk deeper in the earth than the other. …They appear never to have been used, and are of various lengths from six to two inches; they have no shanks, but are in the shape of a triangle, with two long sides." (Atwater, Caleb, *Description of Antiquities Discovered in the State of Ohio and Other Western States*, 1820, pp 137, 139-140)

WINGED BANNER DISTRIBUTION

An interesting note on the distribution of winged bannerstones in Ohio: "…within the Ohio region most notched winged (or butterfly) bannerstones have been found to date within the northwestern quadrant of the state." (Shriver, Phillip R., "An Early Archaic Single-Notched Winged Bannerstone," *Ohio Archaeologist*, Vol. 33 No. 3, Summer 1983, p 26)

OHS ORIGINS

The Ohio Historical Society was formerly the Ohio State Archaeological and Historical Society which was formerly the Archaeological Society. This all began about 120 years ago. "During the year 1875, an Archaeological Society was formed at General Brinkerhoff's house, in Mansfield, Ohio. This Society, through the efforts of Gen. Brinkerhoff, received an appropriation from the State of Ohio of $2,500.00, to make an exhibit at the Exposition at Philadelphia." (Editor, "Monthly Report," *The Archaeologist*, Vol. 3 No. 1, January 1895, p 15)

HANCOCK COUNTY CAVES

Just north of Vanlue in Hancock County, a large hilltop was believed to have had burial caves in limestone rock. In the year 1875, a farmer attempting to dig out fox dens came upon human skeletons about 8 feet below the surface. Several slate pendants were found, also bone tools and a pottery pipe. These suggest a fairly late prehistoric affiliation. (Nissley, J. R., "A Mound-Builder's Cave," *The American Antiquarian*, January 1888, Vol. X No. 1, pp 43-44)

INDIAN ACCOMPLISHMENTS

The following quote could apply to Ohio Hopewell, but might also refer to any Ohio prehistoric group(s): "No primitive people has shown such skill and perseverance in wresting from nature the raw materials needed for their purposes, nor such versatility in fashioning these materials into finished products… we find a vivid picture of the strength and persistence of the forces underlying human development." (Galbreath, Charles B., *History of Ohio*, Vol. I, 1925, p 55)

OHIO CACHES

A cache was found in 1872, in a wetland area of Ashland County, 201 finished specimens recovered in a container made of red elm bark. The cache site had seemingly been marked with two oak stakes and a layer of yellow sand. All artifacts were about ⅜ inch thick and from 3¼ to 4 inches long. In 1877, a Summit County cache was found in a wetland setting, and totaled 197 specimens. The length range was from 2½ to 8½ inches and material was a grey flint. Also in 1877 a large cache of 621 artifacts (plus several dozen fragmentary examples) was plowed out in a Montgomery County orchard. The length range of the artifacts was 2 to 5 inches, and material was a brown-black chert. It was noted that while most were somewhat oval, narrow examples were the longest. (Shepherd, Henry A., *Antiquities of the State of Ohio*, 1887, pp 111-113)

PLUMMET MYSTERY

While it is gradually becoming accepted that most lizard effigies, birdstones and stone or slate gorget types were associated with the Atl-atl, no really plausible use or purpose has turned up for plummets. Cones (along with boatstones) may also have been Atl-atl related, and bar amulets were likely handle-grips, but plummet use remains somewhat of a mystery. The best guess so far is the possibility that plummets were used as thrown weights secured to cords in order to entangle or entrap waterfowl. This could have been done either as a bolas-type arrangement or as anchors for thrown nets. (Hothem, Lar, various sources)

METEORITIC IRON ARTIFACTS

Meteoritic iron is a rare material for artifacts, but it is sometimes found in Ohio mounds of the Hopewell culture. Small pieces, some slightly worked, came from the Turner Mounds; also found were a section of head-plate, hollow beads, and copper ear-ornaments covered with thin meteoritic iron. The most interesting artifact from this Group was the casing for a three-tube pan-pipe about 3½ inches long. The Hopewell Group, Ross County, produced ornaments, an adz blade, a drill or pin, and chisels with antler handles. These chisels were in the shape of beaver teeth. In the Liberty Group, Scioto Valley, were found ear-ornaments and buttons with meteoritic iron coverings and an adz blade. Possibly a knife made of the same material was in the large central mound at Circleville. (Willoughby, Charles C., *The Turner Group of Earthworks / Hamilton County, Ohio*, 1922, pp 50-51, 65-67, Plate 17, figure 21)

WARREN COUNTY BLADE

One of the largest flint artifacts to come from the state of Ohio was found in the Taylor Mound near Oregonia, Warren County. Probably Fort Ancient in origin, the double-pointed blade measured 14⅛ inches long. (Moorehead, Warren K., *Primitive Man in Ohio*, 1892, p 102, figure XLIII)

MOST ANCIENT STRUCTURE

The oldest human-made structure found so far in North America is believed to be in Ohio. It is the remains of a Paleo circular structure in Medina County, dated to ca. 9000 BC. (Matthews, Peter, *The Guinness Book of Records / 1994*, p 241)

ROCK-SHELTER PIPE

Some unusual artifacts have come from rock-shelters in Ohio. One such is a large steatite duck effigy pipe, from Meigs County near the Ohio River. This superb specimen, undoubtedly the finest Ohio great pipe, was found in the year 1853. (Hart, Gordon, "The Greatest of the Great Pipes," *Ohio Archaeologist*, Vol. 31 No. 2, Spring 1981, pp 9-11)

JAMESTOWN EXPOSITION EXHIBIT

In 1907, the state of Ohio sent many prehistoric artifacts to the Jamestown Exposition. The Ohio Exhibit took up some 1800 square feet and included a wide variety of pipes. The following types were in Case No. 15: Tray 1, two frog-effigy pipes, one sandstone from Warren County, one hardstone from Brown County; tray 2, large human effigy, Tuscarawas County, very fine; tray 3, two fine platform pipes, Scioto County; tray 4, three fine pipes, one a bear effigy of a mother defending her cub; tray 5, effigy pipe of a bear's head, duck, hawk and human head; tray 6, miscellaneous pipes of Ohio pipestone and one of hematite; tray 7, platform pipes from Pike and Scioto Counties; tray 8, human effigy pipes from the Miami and Scioto Valleys. (Mills, William C., *Ohio Archaeological Exhibit at the Jamestown Exposition*, 1909(?), pp 39-41)

ROSS COUNTY ADENA BLADE

An exceptional stemmed Adena blade made of mottled Flintridge was found some years ago, probably in Ross County. Length of this fine, wide specimen was 7 inches. (Editor, *Prehistoric Art / Archaeology "80"*, GIRS, Vol. XV No. 1, p 21)

49 — Axe, Miami River full or 4/4 groove, 3³/₄ x 4¹/₄ inches. Ex-collection Bapst, this Archaic axe in dark hardstone with good polish is from Delaware County. Fred Winegardner collection, Ohio

50 — Axe, full or 4/4 groove, Archaic, 5¹/₄ x 8¹/₈ inches. Material is grey hardstone and the axe is well-shaped and has a highly polished blade area. Fairfield County. Herbert M. Turner collection, Ohio

51 — Axe, 3/4 groove, Archaic, 5¼ inches high. It is made of mixed colored hardstone and has excellent lines and is in top condition. Van Wert County. Spahr collection, Ohio

52 — Axe, 3/4 groove, Archaic period, 5 inches high. Material is speckled hardstone and the piece is highly polished overall. Hocking County. Fred Winegardner collection, Ohio

53 — Axe, 3/4–4/4 groove, 4¼ inches high. Well-polished in the groove area, this Archaic axe with groove characteristics of two types is ex-collection Chadwick and came from Union County. Fred Wine-gardner collection, Ohio

54 — Axe, 4/4 groove, 4⅜ inches high. With good polish remaining, this Miami River type axe in dark hardstone is from Knox County. Fred Wine-gardner collection

55 — *Axe, Archaic period, 3/4–4/4 groove, 5¼ inches high. This axe in dark speckled hardstone is ex-collection Johnson and came from Delaware County. Fred Winegardner collection, Ohio*

56 — *Axe, 3/4 groove, Archaic, 8¼ inches high. Material is a yellow-tan hardstone for this large axe which has excellent lines. Vinton County. Spahr collection, Ohio*

57 — Axe, 3/4 groove, Archaic, 7 inches high. It is made of brown hardstone with mica sparkles and is a very well-formed artifact. It came from Perry County. Spahr collection, Ohio

58 — Axe, Archaic, 3/4 groove, 7⅝ inches high. Greenish hardstone is the material for this high-grooved example with crisp lines. Wayne County. Spahr collection, Ohio

59 — *Axe, 3/4 groove, Archaic, 6¾ inches high. Well-polished, it is made of yellow-tan hardstone and came from Van Wert County. Spahr collection, Ohio*

60 — *Axe, 3/4 groove, Archaic, 5½ inches high. Material is a dark hardstone with lighter-colored inclusions and the 1/4 side is nicely fluted. Darke County. Spahr collection, Ohio*

61 — Axe, 3/4 groove, Archaic, 7½ inches high. Made of mottled dark and light hardstone this piece has high overall polish and came from Hancock County. Spahr collection, Ohio

62 — Axe, full or 4/4 groove, Archaic, 4½ inches high. Made of brown hardstone, this high-grooved example is ex-collection E.R. Davis and is marked "1949." Champaign County. Fred Winegardner collection, Ohio

63 — *Axe, 3/4 groove, Archaic, 8¼ inches high. This is a well-shaped axe with a wide groove, made of unusual material, quartzite. Defiance County. Spahr collection, Ohio*

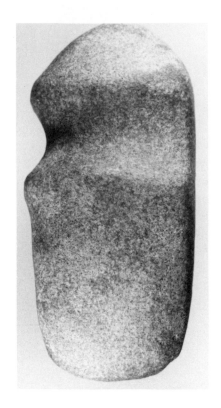

64 — *Axe, 3/4 groove, Archaic, 6¼ inches high. This is a sturdy and well-designed axe made of blue-grey hardstone. Preble County. Larry Garvin,* **Back to Earth**, *Ohio*

65 — Bell pestle, Archaic period, with basal diameter of 3⅜ inches and 4¾ inches high. It is made of tan hardstone, is in undamaged condition, and from Fairfield County. Herbert M. Turner collection, Ohio

66 — Club-head(?), full or 4/4 groove, Archaic, 4 inches high. A rare raised-groove example, it is made of dark hardstone and is well-polished. Ex-collection Tolliver, it came from Hocking County. Fred Winegardner collection, Ohio

67 — *Hammerstone, 3/4 groove, Archaic period, 3 inches high. Well-made hammerstones like this are actually not a common artifact in the state. Worked in dark speckled hardstone, this artifact is from Ohio, county unknown. Spahr collection, Ohio*

68 — *Club-head(?), full groove, Archaic, 3 inches high. It has good polish above and below the groove area. Ex-collection Tolliver, it came from Hocking County. Larry Garvin,* **Back to Earth**, *Ohio*

69 — Two small Archaic axes, both Ohio. Left, 4/4 groove, 2⅞ inches high, green hardstone, county unknown. Right, 3/4 groove, 3⅜ inches high, nicely polished, Montgomery County. Fred Winegardner collection, Ohio

70 — Two miniature Archaic axes, 3/4 grooved. Left, 2½ inches, tan hardstone, Shelby County. Right, 2¼ inches high, dark polished hardstone, Delaware County. Fred Winegardner collection, Ohio

71 — Two miniature Archaic axes, 3/4 grooved; both are from Fairfield County. Left, 3 inches, grey-green hardstone. Right, 3⅛ inches, polished groove, also grey-green hardstone. Herbert M. Turner collection, Ohio

72 — Gouge, Archaic period, 6 inches long. Gouges are quite scarce in Ohio and are rarely found, at least prime pieces in top condition. Material is yellow-tan hardstone and the artifact is from Franklin County. Fred Winegardner collection, Ohio

73 — Pestle, bell type, Archaic, 5³⁄₈ inches high. This piece has crisp, clean lines and is made of tan hardstone. Fairfield County. Herbert M. Turner collection, Ohio

74 — Pestle, bell type, Archaic period, 3¹⁄₂ x 4³⁄₄ inches. Made of yellow and orange hardstone, this tool was found near Baltic, Tuscarawas County. Spahr collection, Ohio

75 — Celt, Woodland period, 4 inches long. Probably Adena in origin, material is brown hardstone and the celt is Ohio, county unknown. Spahr collection, Ohio

76 — Celt, Adena and Early Woodland period, 2⅛ x 5³/₁₆ inches. It is made of grey hardstone with black spotting, has medium polish, and came from Richland County. Lar Hothem collection, Ohio

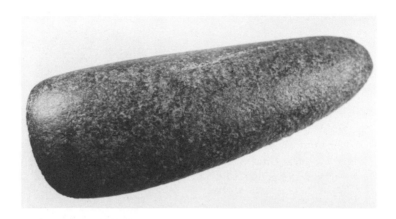

77 — Adz, triangular Adena shape and Early Woodland, 5⅞ inches long. Made of brown hardstone, it is well-polished. Ex-collection Tolliver, Hocking County. Fred Winegardner collection, Ohio

78 — Celt, Woodland period and probably Adena, 5¾ inches long. Made of dark hardstone, this celt is well-shaped and heavily polished overall. Ex-collection Hupp, it is from Licking County. Fred Winegardner collection, Ohio

79 — Celt, Hopewell squared-poll type, 5³⁄₈ inches long. Middle Woodland period, it is nicely polished in dark hardstone. Richland County. Fred Winegardner collection, Ohio

80 — Chisel, Mississippian period, 5¹⁄₂ inches long. Highly polished, this narrow celt-like tool is round in cross-section and ex-collection Kohr. It is from Tuscarawas County. Spahr collection, Ohio

Miami Valley pottery

Not a great deal has been written about the prehistoric pottery of Ohio. Fort Ancient examples of the Miami Valley, however, have been summarized: "The prevailing type of vessel is a round-bodied pot with wide mouth and flaring rim. Deep bowls are occasionally seen. The pots are strongly characterized by their handles, which connect the lip with the shoulder. As a rule these handles are thin bands, and lie close to the neck of the vessel. Their number is usually four, but two are sometimes seen, and occasionally these are more than four. In most cases they are wider where they join the rim, which is often drawn out to meet them. The outer surface of the handles is plain and flat in most cases, but examples occur in which it is concave, and in rather rare instances it is round. In no other section do handles form so important a feature of the ware as in southwestern Ohio." (Holmes, W. H., "Aboriginal Pottery of Eastern United States," *20th Annual Report of the Bureau of American Ethnology*, 1903, pp 184-185)

Intrusive Mound artifacts

The Intrusive Mound people of Late Woodland times had a number of artifacts that were different enough to make the culture distinctive when considered as a whole. Artifacts include: Hardstone celts; chipped and polished flint celts; stone gouges; large nodular flint scrapers or cutters; angular flint arrowheads; antler tool handles; antler hammers or clubs; antler gouges; bone beamers; platform pipes, plain and effigy; ceremonial picks rounded or squared in cross-section; antler tools with inset beaver teeth; bone and antler barbed harpoons; slate pendants; bone spatula-like tools; bone awls or needles; antler arrow-tips; and, unworked pieces of bone and antler. (Mills, William C., "Exploration of the Mound City Group," *Certain Mounds and Village Sites in Ohio*, Vol. 3 Part 4, 1922, pp 386-406)

Early Dealer Advertisement

At one time artifact collectors and dealers were scattered across Ohio, in towns large and small; some of the villages are now gone forever. "Flint, Slate and Stone Indian relics, nearly 3000 PERFECT SPECIMENS. Send for pricelist. Get something really good from Central Ohio. Address Z. X. Corey, Phirisburg, O." (Advertisement, *The Archaeologist*, Vol. 2 No. 1, January 1894, last page)

Wisconsin or Ohio

Dr. I. A. Lapham, pioneer archaeologist and engineer / surveyor for the state of Wisconsin, might—but for a twist of fate—have been one of the founders of Ohio archaeology. "In 1836, Dr. Lapham lost his position as Secretary of the State Board of Public Works at Columbus, Ohio, owing to a change of the party in power, and immediately decided to 'go West.'" (Lapham, Mary J., "Dr. Increase A. Lapham," *The Wisconsin Archaeologist*, Vol. 1 No. 2, January 1902, p 32)

High-grade Upper Mercer

While most people are familiar with the colors and grades of Flintridge material, the Warsaw quarries (Coshocton flint, Upper Mercer) also produced some near-gem grades. And, the "translucency test" used to identify Flintridge may not always be significant. The Warsaw quarries: "There is much variety in the quality and appearance of the flint at this place. Part of it is cellular, almost spongy, from the weathering out of fossils and various impurities. By insensible graduations it passes into stone as compact and homogeneous as fine agate. Seams of chalcedony, and cavities filled or lined with quartz crystals, occur abundantly. Chert, glossy basanite, and small masses of chalcedony are common. The color runs through various shades of white, black, blue and red, and there is also the pale amber or 'honey color,' very rare in this country. Some is almost transparent, and from this it merges into complete opacity." (Fowke, Gerard, *Archaeological History of Ohio*, 1902, pp 624-625)

GLACIAL KAME SHELL GORGETS

Three large Glacial Kame sandal-sole shell gorgets have come from Ohio. Sizes and county provenance: 2¼ x 8½ inches, Putnam County; 2⅞ x 9⅛ inches, Mercer County; and, 2⅞ x 9½ inches, also Mercer County. (Cunningham, Wilbur M., *A Study of the Glacial Kame Culture*, 1948, pp 21-22, plate VI)

MOUND GOLD

Silver in any form is considered a rarity in Ohio mounds, and gold is probably unique. Yet, some gold was found in Mound Three of the Hopewellian Turner Group, Hamilton County. Native gold nuggets had been pounded into small, irregular sheets. There were 15 in all, one of which was adhered to a holed pendant or dangle made of copper. (Willoughby, Charles C., *The Turner Group of Earthworks / Hamilton County, Ohio*, 1922, p 52, plates 11 & 13)

MONTGOMERY COUNTY CACHE

Cache reports for Ohio are sometimes found in obscure publications, and one such is included here: "Old 'Uncle Binkley' who once lived near Alexanderville, in Montgomery County, Ohio, and was the owner of the land where a large circle of earthwork indicated an entrenched camp of the Mound Builders, found a deposit of six hundred leaf shaped arrow points. They were evenly and beautifully made, and complete, save the placing of the 'nock' or notch for the sinew attachment to the shaft of the arrow." (Kern, Albert, "Fort Ancient—A Pre-Historic Fortification," *The Ohio Magazine*, 1907, p 213)

SQUIER AND DAVIS

Ephraim G. Squier and Dr. Edwin H. Davis are famous for

co-authoring the 1848 Smithsonian publication, *Ancient Monuments of the Mississippi Valley*, which covered many of Ohio's major earthworks. Hence, some facts about the two should be of interest. "Mr. Davis was a native of Chillicothe, and was then about 35 years of age. He was a reserved and somewhat diffident gentleman; and of the highest character. ...Mr. Squier was an entirely different man. He had come from the East to assist in editing the Scioto *Gazette*. He was then about 26 years of age, blonde, small and boyish in figure, but one of the most audacious, inspiring figures... He had a talent for management, and not withstanding his insignificant presence could make his way everywhere." After seeing some of the earthworks, Squier asked a friend if anyone else had an attachment for such things. Squier and Davis worked together, with Davis furnishing the funds. After publication of their work, Davis studied the archaeology of New York state and Squier received a governmental appointment to Central America where he investigated ancient sites. Having cooperated so much before, both men died in the same year, 1887. (Howe, Henry, *Historical Collections of Ohio*, Vol. II, 1896, p 510)

INCISED MOUTH BIRDSTONES

Most birdstones lack facial features, but a small percentage have had such extra design work. "Studies made of more than 1000 birdstones show that 10.7% of them have incised mouths. Of those examples, approximately 51.9% fall into the flat, stubby class." (Tiell, William, "The Incised Mouth Birdstones," *Ohio Archaeologist*, Vol. 25 No. 3, Summer 1975, pp 20-21)

ADENA ADZ

A large Adena adz was found in Coshocton County in 1963. Made of well-polished green hardstone, the adz measured 2⅝ x 1⅛ x 8 inches long. (Editor, *Ohio Archaeologist*, Vol. 14 No. 2, April 1964, p 55)

Hardin County Glacial Kame

The Zimmerman Site was one of the major Glacial Kame (Late Archaic) locations in Ohio. In Hardin County, explorations were begun in 1931 with the taking of gravel from a knoll. The Doctor Bondley collection from this site included 13 sandal-sole gorgets or portions of gorgets (one engraved), 6 two-hole gorgets (one with a snake design), 144 copper beads, a slate tube 6½ inches long, plus other minor artifacts. (Cunningham, Wilbur M., *A Study of the Glacial Kame Culture*, 1948, pp 10-12, plate VIII)

Hocking Valley rock-shelters

Very little has been written about the many large "dry caves" or rock shelters in Ohio. Some work, however, was done about a century ago. "In the Hocking [River] region the sand and dirt was [sic] scooped out of many of the caves, and although pieces of pottery and arrow heads and other flint implements were found in several caverns, there was no indication that more than one of the Hocking caves have been inhabited in glacial times. At Ash Cave we found a cavern some 80 feet in height, 100 feet in depth and 400 feet long. Two hundred and fifty feet of this distance is covered by a deposit of ashes, ranging from 2 to 6 feet in depth. Picnic parties, relic collectors and others have pretty well dug over the entire deposit." (Moorehead, Warren K., "Preliminary Exploration of Ohio Caves," *The Archaeologist*, Vol. 3 No. 9, September 1895, p 311)

Cupstone theory

Cupstones or nutstones are familiar to every collector and amateur archaeologist, and very many supposed uses have been assigned to them. There is some proof for a single use, as the following account suggests: "Dr. Rau reports that some of the specimens in the Smithsonian collection still show traces of red paint in the cavities, and it is possible they were generally used to grind down pieces of hematite for paint." (Read, Matthew C., *Archaeology of Ohio*, 1888, p 39)

OHIO GLACIAL BOUNDARY

The boundary that establishes the limits of glaciation in Ohio is important for two reasons. Broadly considered, and with exceptions, prehistoric peoples preferred the more gentled landscape of glaciated areas. Also, glacial deposits of hardstone and slate meant the ready availability of raw materials for tools and ornaments. The glacial terminals in Ohio: "Entering Ohio in Columbiana County, about ten miles north of the Ohio River, the glacial boundary runs westward through New Lisbon to Canton in Stark County, and thence to Millersburg in Holmes County. A few miles west of this place it turns abruptly south, passing through Danville in Knox County, Newark in Licking County, Lancaster in Fairfield County, to Adelphi in Ross County. Thence bearing more westward it passes through Chillicothe to southeastern Highland County and northwestern Adams, reaching the Ohio River near Ripley, in Clermont County. Thence, following the north bank of the Ohio River to Cincinnati, it crosses the river." (Wright, G. Frederick, *Man and the Glacial Period*, 1896, p 95)

OHIO HERITAGE

It is always instructive to receive objective summaries of Ohio's prehistoric artifacts, even when such comments were made years ago. The richness of this state's heritage is verified time and again: "Our collection, in which no attempt has been made to segregate the culture, illustrates the remarkable variety and superior workmanship which characterizes the stone art of Ohio as a whole, qualities seen mainly in the pipes and problematic forms—bannerstones, gorgets, bird-stones, and the like." (Hodge, F. W., *Indian Notes and Monographs / Guide to the Museum - Second Floor*, Museum of the American Indian, Heye Foundation, 1922, pp 168-169)

MIAMI RIVER AXES

Ohio has long been noted as a state with high-quality axes.

An example is the full-groove Miami River axe which is found mainly in southwestern Ohio. This axe is unusual, most specimens appearing top-heavy. "Named by Dr. Meuser, and also called the 'Ohio Axe,' the poll is sometimes well-made, rounded and symmetrical. The blade tapers to a bit that is smaller than the rest of the blade. The taper can be slight or very pronounced." (Henderson, Charles F., "Some Examples of the Miami River Axe," *Ohio Archaeologist*, Vol. 45 No. 3, Summer 1995, p 9)

HAMILTON COUNTY MOUND ATTRACTION

One of the larger Adena mounds in Ohio was the Martin Mound, also known as the Walker Mound. Located in Hamilton County the mound was 625 feet in circumference, 250 feet in diameter, and 39 feet high. During the Depression years of the 1930s, a man dug tunnels into the structure, put in wiring and lights, and opened a walk-in tourist attraction. The mound was eventually destroyed by gravel-mining operations. One artifact known to have come from the Martin Mound was a tubular pipe with "...a bird-like pattern." (Starr, S. Frederick, *The Archaeology of Hamilton County, Ohio*, 1960, p 57)

ARTIFACTS PAID ADVERTISING

The Archaeologist, published in Columbus, Ohio, in the 1890s, like many businesses at the time seems to have had a shortage of ready cash. "*The Archaeologist* has a small collection of choice relics which were taken in payment for advertising. It offers to the highest cash bidder the lot. Hematite plumb bob, tube, tube pipe, slate ornament, 150 assorted flint implements, 21 axes, pestles and celts, ceremonial, gouge, elongated pestle, 5 whole Arkansas bowls and jars. Bids close September 1st. F. Brown, manager, Box 502, Columbus, O." ("Notice / Collectors Department," *The Archaeologist*, Vol. 3 No. 8, August 1895, p 292)

OHIO PREHISTORIC WORKS

Ohio's quantitative position in prehistory considered: "The territory embraced within the State of Ohio probably contains a greater number of prehistoric remains than any other equal area in the Mississippi valley." (Mills, William C., *Archeological Atlas of Ohio*, 1914, p III)

OHIO BASIC BANNERSTONE

The one bannerstone type that may have a range center mainly in Ohio is the Humped (Type No. 1). This basic form has a flattened base or bottom, a curved top and sides, and the length is greater than width. While the type is distributed into surrounding states, Ohio is the only state geographic region that appears to be solidly covered. (Knoblock, Byron W., *Bannerstones of the North American Indian*, 1939, p 159)

EARLY DEALER ADVERTISEMENT

Another of the state's early artifact dealers advertised his offerings. "Spearheads: 2 small, 2 med., 2 large, 2 bird, 2 game, 2 war points, 2 wampum — 14 fine, whole ancient relics, 92 (cents) p.p.; cat. 100 illus., 10 [cents], free with order. J. R. Nissley, Ada, Ohio." (Advertisement, *The Archaeologist*, Vol. 3 No. 3, March 1895)

ASHLAND COUNTY TROPHY AXE

Ashland County, about 1963, produced a fine and rare Ohio trophy axe. The full-grooved specimen of tan gneiss had grey and black banding and the typical unsharpened bit. The axe height was 5 inches. (Goard, George Jr., "Trophy Axe from Ashland County," *Ohio Archaeologist*, Vol. 32 No. 2, Spring 1982, p 9)

MOUND REDUCTION RATE

Early cultivation of Ohio mounds reduced the heights (and

increased the circumferences) of mounds to varying degrees, depending on location, type of soil, original height, weathering, frequency of cultivation, etc. An average figure might be a reduction in height of about 1½ feet (18 inches) every decade (10 years). (Hothem, Lar, various sources)

OHIO BIRDSTONE AREA

Birdstone distribution in the state of Ohio was briefly and generally summarized nearly 40 years ago. "…it can be said that if a line be drawn from Cincinnati in southwestern Ohio to Conneaut in northeastern Ohio, that the predominate amount of birdstones are found northwesterly of that line." (Johnston, LaDow, *Ohio Archaeologist / Ohio Indian Relic Collectors Society*, July 1954, p 17)

HOPEWELL AND MODERN CENTERS

Many Ohio cities today are located where the Hopewell people (Middle Woodland) erected their own major groupings of earthworks. These include the cities of Chillicothe, Cincinnati, Circleville, Marietta, Newark, and Portsmouth. A commonality of all these sites is location at or near the confluence of several streams (Chillicothe, Circleville, Newark) or the confluence of a large stream with one still larger (Cincinnati, Marietta, Portsmouth). This suggests the importance of creeks and rivers in Hopewell times, probably as much for transportation, trade and communication as for the usual other reasons. (Hothem, Lar, various sources)

MERCER COUNTY ADENA CACHE

A cache of corner-notched Adena points or blade was found in Mercer County in 1987. There were 75 fragmentary and whole specimens made of a grey to white chert. Sizes of the artifacts ranged from 1½ to 3⅞ inches long. (Street, Larry, "A Mercer County Cache," *Ohio Archaeologist*, Vol. 39 No. 2, Spring 1989, p 21)

Ohio Indian Relic Collectors Society

The Ohio Indian Relic Collectors Society, of Columbus, was the predecessor of the current Archaeological Society of Ohio. The credo of the early group was easily stated: "Object Of The Society / To preserve archaeological sites and specimens, and to bring about a closer relationship between the collector and the archaeologist." (*Ohio Indian Relic Collectors Society*, Bulletin No. 12, February 1945)

Holmes County cache

Even more than a century ago, when interest in prehistoric Ohio artifacts was rather thinly spread, reports of caches attracted attention: "An interesting 'find' of flint implements of the leaf-shaped pattern was discovered in the summer of 1870 on the farm of Daniel Kick, about half a mile north of the Lake Fork of Mohican River, in Washington Township, Holmes County, Ohio. They were found in a pond or basin-like depression formed in the glacial drift or river gravel which is found in this vicinity. The pond has no outlet, as the rim of the basin is 20 feet high. In order to collect the water, which, during most seasons, covers the bottom of the pond, a ditch 4 feet deep was dug through it. Near the bottom of the ditch were found the remains of an old oak log lying across the cutting, and beside the log were found ninety-six flint implements, all leaf-shaped, and of sizes from 2¼ to 5½ inches in length. They were colored by red oxide of iron, which adhered very tenaciously to the flint, showing that a quantity of this material had been deposited with them. This pond, in seasons of great drought, becomes dry, but has not been so for several years." (Case, H. B., "Flint Implements in Holmes County, Ohio / Antiquities of Ohio," *Annual Report of the Board of Regents of the Smithsonian Institution / 1877*, 1878, p 267)

Collections and finances

While we may feel financial times in recent years have been

difficult, apparently money problems were considerably worse a century and more ago, especially in regard to artifact collections. "Never in the history of Archaeology in this country have there been more offered for sale than are on the market at present. The Editor does not refer to the offers of dealers, but to old collectors, who, having felt the financial depression, are anxious to dispose of their cabinets at a figure less than the original cost. ...We have in mind seventeen cabinets which can be bought at prices ranging from two hundred to two thousand dollars. Many of these are the results of a life's labor." (Moorehead, Warren K., "Editorial," *The Archaeologist*, Vol. 3 No. 3, March 1895, p 97)

Intrusive Mound pipe

An outstanding Late Woodland platform pipe (Intrusive Mound people) was found near Manchester, Adams County, in 1830. Made of highly polished black steatite, the platform pipe had a high rounded bowl with a squared top. A human face was relief-carved on the bowl side facing the smoker. This rare pipe was 4½ inches high and 9 inches long. (Grimm, Robert E., *Prehistoric Art*, 1953, pp 134-135)

Ross County tubular pipe

Perhaps the finest Adena plain tubular pipe to come from Ohio was found in a mound near Chillicothe, Ross County. Made of glacial slate, the color was brownish to lead-green with bands of black, and the pipe was well-polished. The pipe was $1\frac{1}{10}$ inches in diameter and 13 inches long. One end expanded slightly and the mouthpiece end had a wide, flat triangular flare "...of fine proportions, which is carved with mathematical precision." Fully drilled, the interior hole was $\frac{7}{10}$ inches across, which size was abruptly reduced to $\frac{1}{10}$ inch at the mouthpiece. (Squier, Ephraim G., and E. H. Davis, *Ancient Monuments of the Mississippi Valley*, 1848, p 224)

HIGHLAND COUNTY ADVERTISEMENT

Classified advertisement for artifacts placed over a century ago: "Some very valuable banner stones, ceremonials, gorgets, etc., for sale cheap. Warren Cowen, Elmville, Highland County, Ohio." ("Exchange Department," *The Archaeologist*, Vol. 2 No. 11, November 1894, p 350)

ROSS COUNTY HILLTOP ENCLOSURE

There are a number of Hopewell fortified hilltops in Ohio, especially in the southwestern portion of the state. Spruce Hill Fort, in Ross County, has an added distinction: "This fort is probably the largest area in the world surrounded by an artificial wall made entirely of stone." (Fowke, Gerard, *Archaeological History of Ohio*, 1902, p 244)

MONTGOMERY COUNTY ADENA BLADE

One of the finest Adena blades came from Montgomery County, and was found in close proximity to several caches of leaf-shaped artifacts. "...the most extraordinary specimen in the whole lot, however, is a cream-colored leaf-shaped blade made of Flint Ridge chalcedony, ten inches in length and three inches in breadth." (Mills, William C., "The Ulrich Group of Mounds," *Ohio Archaeological & Historical Society Publications*, Vol. XXVIII, 1919, pp 163-164)

PERRY COUNTY HILLTOP ENCLOSURE

The Glenford Stone Fort, also called the Glenford Fort, is located in northern Perry County. It is typical of several major hilltop fortifications or stoneworks in central and southern Ohio. The wall is formed of sandstone blocks, with a total length of about 6610 feet. An area of approximately 26 acres was enclosed and a large stone mound is located near the center. The site, apparently first reported by Caleb Atwater in 1820, has long been considered a Hopewell creation. However, in the past several years excavations indicate that the mound at least was erected by the Adena, an Early Woodland people. Fine stemmed blades have been recovered, plus pottery shards and a pottery short-tube pipe, proof of Adena presence. Studies continue as to the origin of the wall itself. (Hothem, Lar, personal communication, Jim Dutcher, 18Oct1992)

OLD STATE MUSEUM DISPLAYS

Some readers will remember the State Museum on North High Street in Columbus, beside the main entrance to The Ohio State University. Part of a description of the displays is included here. "Aside from holding more than an average number of specimens from a distance, the Buckeye Historical Society has as complete a line of local artifacts as I have ever laid my eyes upon. In it is a case of mortars and pestles of various sizes and types, all showing signs of much labor, and some are symmetrical and well-polished. There are ornaments, plain and fancy, of mica and copper; ceremonials of slate and bannerstone; fragments of Mound Builders' cloth framed in glass... and pipes of every description... There is a well assorted collection of implements and ornaments made from the bone and bear teeth that range from the large celt to the delicate fish hook; also copper spuds and plates." (Editor, *The Archaeological Bulletin*, January-February 1915, Vol. 6 No. 1, p 17)

ANTIQUES AND ANTIQUITIES

Warren K. Moorehead, famed author, lecturer, excavator, and foremost archaeologist of the time, was also upon occasion somewhat of an antiques dealer. "A large German serving tray of 1799, valued at $25, a fine Grandfather's clock, 8 feet high (made in 1765) in good condition and valued at $100 to exchange for Indian relics or cash. W. K. Moorehead, Box 502, Columbus, O." ("Exchange Department," *The Archaeologist*, Vol. 2 No. 12, December 1894, p 384)

WYANDOT COUNTY PALEO POINT

One of the rarest projectile point tips was recently found in northern Ohio. This was recovered in a pit near Indian Trail Cavern close to Fostoria on 16Jul1995. The Wyandot County bone or antler tip was 5 inches long, and of a type known as "pin spear." It is probably from the Paleo period, possibly ca. 9500 BC. [Such points are often narrow pointed cylinders, with one end terminating in a flat bevel, sometimes with incised cross-hatching.] ("Discovery of Unique Relic May Keep Ancient Pit Open", *The Columbus Dispatch*, 2Aug1995)

OHIO AXE NOTES

An observation about Ohio axes is worth being emphasized: "For the most part, grooved axes found in Ohio are made of the tough, hard granite boulders brought down by the drift and the finest specimens are found in the Miami and Scioto Valleys." (Mills, William C., *Ohio Archaeological Exhibit at the Jamestown Exposition*, 1909(?), p 46)

ADENA LACKED OBSIDIAN

While obsidian in the form of artifacts, raw material or flakes has been found in many Hopewell mounds, the same is not true of Adena mounds. "One of the more interesting facets of the distribution of obsidian in the Ohio Valley and its temporal position is that there is only one known identification of it from sites attributed to the Adena culture. One might not expect to find obsidian in the earlier Adena sites, but in the later sites with a cultural and radiocarbon overlap with Ohio Hopewell, it would not be surprising to find some obsidian. ...It can safely be stated, however, that as far as is now known, obsidian was not available during the period of construction of Adena mounds or of the occupation of Adena villages." (Griffin, James B., "Hopewell and the Dark Black Glass," *Michigan Archaeologist*, 1965, Vol. II Nos. 3 & 4, p 129)

HOPEWELL PLATFORM PIPE DISTRIBUTION

Hopewell platform-type pipes may have a distribution center in southwestern Ohio, one wider than commonly known. "This type exists in Illinois, Indiana, Michigan, Wisconsin, West Virginia, Kentucky, and rarely in Tennessee, Eastern Missouri and Arkansas. It seems confined to a region three hundred and fifty miles in diameter, having Cincinnati as its center." (Moorehead, Warren K., "Information for Collectors," *The Archaeologist*, Vol. 2 No. 7, July 1894, p 224)

LORAIN COUNTY STEMMED BLADE

One of the largest stemmed blades found in Ohio came from Lorain County. It was found by the Garfield family in 1837, when a basement was being excavated. The blade was made of light grey flint and measured 2¼ inches wide and 10⅛ inches long. (Vietzen, Col. Raymond C., *Indians of the Lake Erie Basin*, 1965, pp 62-63, 255)

RECORD OHIO SITES

The state of Ohio has many "firsts," including quite a few examples from prehistoric times. "Ohio is fortunate in having, however, in the Great Serpent Mound, the most impressive of the effigy tumuli on the continent; the tallest of the conical mounds in the Miamisburg Mound; and the most striking defensive earthwork in the noted Fort Ancient." (Shetrone, Henry C., "The Ohio Aborigines," *The History of the State of Ohio*, Vol. I, 1941, p 51)

GUERNSEY COUNTY MOUND

One of Ohio's largest mounds is (or was) in Guernsey County. "Mound 53 feet high (elliptical), 10 miles south of Cambridge, 1 mile from Point Pleasant." (Thomas, Cyrus, *Catalogue of Prehistoric Works East of the Rocky Mountains*, Smithsonian, 1891, p 173)

OHIO ARTIFACT ADVERTISEMENTS

Ohioans have always been somewhat enterprising when prehistoric artifacts are concerned. "Wanted to Exchange — Trilobites… for arrow-heads or Indian relics of any kind. W. T. Hambidge, Eaton, Ohio." (and) "Stamps from all over the world to exchange for Indian relics. Send list. C. Krug, Forestville, Ohio." (and) "A typical collection of Southern Ohio relics for exchange or sale; 450 specimens; all good. Address, Warren K. Moorehead, box 502, Columbus, O." ("Exchange Department," *The Archaeologist*, Vol. 2 No. 10, October 1894)

OHIO MOUND CULTURES

When one thinks of mounds in Ohio, those of Early and Middle Woodland times (Adena and Hopewell) come immediately to mind. The state, however, had five major or minor mound-building peoples. They were: Adena, Red Ochre, Hopewell, Cole, and several Mississippian groups of late prehistoric times. (Hothem, Lar, various sources)

ADAMS COUNTY CACHE

A cache of Buck Creek (ca. 1000 BC) points or blades was found near Sulphur Creek, Adams County, Ohio. Well-shaped and quite thin, length of the seven specimens ranged to 5½ inches. (*Atkinson Catalog*, Old Barn Auction, 27Jun1992, p 19)

COUNTY TYPE NAMES

Two well-known prehistoric chipped flint point or blade types are named after Ohio counties. One is the notched/stemmed Ashtabula, Late Archaic / Early Woodland. Another is the Ross, a fluted Early Paleo type. (Hothem, Lar, *Indian Flints of Ohio*, 1986, pp 5, 42)

QUESTIONABLE FIND

Several Ohio artifacts are of interest that were recovered

from the Sparks Mound along the Wilmington-Harveysburg road in Clinton County. The mound was 40 by 45 feet, and 6½ feet high. One artifact was authentic, an Adena formal tablet. The other object was an Archaic butterfly type winged bannerstone, which itself may have been authentic. However, it was highly engraved on both faces with non-Indian figures. One side had a male figure carrying an axe and spear, plus an ornate panel with 20 windows, each with an unusual design. The opposite side had a female figure, and three creatures resembling a cat, an alligator and a snake. This "find" created much publicity and controversy, with many people accepting the pictorial banner as totally original and old. (Welch, Dr. L. B. and J. M. Richardson, *An Illustrated Description of Pre-Historic Relics Found Near Wilmington, Ohio*, 1879, pp 1-7)

LANCEOLATE CACHE

An unusual cache of Late Paleo lanceolate points or blades was found south of Elyria, Ohio, ca. 1870. There was a total of 48 specimens, some slightly shouldered, and all were over 4 inches long. Materials included dark grey Coshocton flint and light grey Nellie flint. (Editor, "Addendum," *Ohio Archaeologist*, Vol. 14 No. 1, January 1964, pp 16-17)

NEWARK EARTHWORK REMOVALS

The Newark Earthworks are famous world-wide, and are known for their fine state of preservation. Over the years, unfortunately, modern civilization encroached in major ways. "When Mr. Atwater first surveyed, or rather had these works surveyed by Judge Holmes (who was a competent surveyor) more than sixty years ago [ca. 1820]—they still being in the wilderness—the aforesaid watchtowers or small mounds of observation, were yet so plainly observable that he located them on his map or engraving of these ancient works. But they and many others are gone, entirely obliterated. Some disappeared when the Ohio Canal was run through this group of ancient works, in 1827; others were destroyed thirty years [ca. 1850] ago, when the road bed of the Central Ohio Railroad was constructed, which runs for a mile or more through this triangle of ancient earthworks; a number more were demolished within a few years, during the progress of the erection of extensive buildings for rolling-mill purposes; and others, many others, as well as low banks or parallel connecting walls or embankments, and small observatories, have disappeared under the long-continued ravages of the plow." (Smucker, Isaac, *Mound Builders' Works Near Newark, Ohio*, 1881, pp 7-8)

FRANKLIN COUNTY PIPE

Little is known about some artifact discoveries of long ago, such as this example: "A fine owl effigy pipe weighing five pounds was presented to the Department of Archaeology of the Ohio State University. It was found near Columbus." (Editor, "Recent Discoveries," *The Archaeologist*, Vol. 2 No. 10, October 1894, p 316)

OHIO INTRUSIVE MOUND CULTURE

Relatively little is known of the so-called Intrusive Mound people in Ohio. "An 'intrusive' culture, probably from north of the Lakes, frequently occurs superimposed in Hopewell and Adena tumuli. The carriers of this culture appear to have entered Ohio at the north and to have proceeded down the Scioto Valley to the Ohio. Recognizing the existing mounds as burial places, they simply dug graves therein for their dead. Their culture is characterized by barbed bone harpoons, tools made by setting beaver teeth transversely through sections of deer antler, straight-based platform tobacco pipes and some others." (Shetrone, Henry C., "The Ohio Aborigines," *The History of the State of Ohio*, Vol. I, 1941, p 53)

MARIETTA PREHISTORIC WELL

Caleb Atwater described the earthworks at Marietta as including a circular cistern or well about 25 feet across and with a raised earthen circumference. "It was, undoubtedly, at first, very deep, as, since its discovery by the first settlers, they have frequently thrust poles into it to the depth of thirty feet. It appears to run to a point, like an inverted cone or funnel and was undoubtedly that kind of well used by the inhabitants of the old world, which were so large at their top as to afford an easy descent down to the fountain, and up again with its water in a vessel borne on the shoulder, according to the ancient custom." (Priest, Josiah, "Vast Works of the Ancient Nations on the East Side of the Muskingum," *Prehistoric Antiquities Quarterly*, Vol. XIII Qtr. 1, February 1993, p 2)

OHIO BIRDSTONE REGIONS

While all of Ohio is well within the distribution area of birdstones, there are actually three regions of find-concentrations. The major area is all of northwestern Ohio. A minor band stretches from this east along the southern shoreline of Lake Erie about to the Pennsylvania border. An isolated additional region is in southern Ohio, and consists of the watershed region of the Scioto River. (Townsend, Earl C. Jr., *Birdstones of the North American Indian*, 1959, p 311, plate 97)

OHIO HILLTOP ENCLOSURES

A brief summary of minor hilltop enclosures in Ohio was given just over a century ago, and the description has value today. Regarding these enclosures: "...there are many small, tolerably regular, circular, square, and elliptical enclosures, found in nearly all portions of the state, often on top of the highest hills. They are from fifty to two hundred feet across, some scarcely traceable, others having an elevation of two or three feet, with a breadth of five to ten times the height. There is but one entrance way, on the east side in most, sometimes on the north or south, very seldom on the west. ...With some, mounds are associated; others are miles from the nearest aboriginal structures." (Fowke, Gerard, *Geological Survey of Ohio—Archaeology*, 1893, Vol. VII, p 14)

TUNNELS THROUGH TIME

Ohio mounds large enough to have been explored by tunneling included the following: The Harness Mound, Ross County; the Carriage Factory Mound, Ross County, diameter 225 feet, height 35 feet; the Story Mound, Ross County; the Roberts Mound, Perry County; and, the Wilson Mound, Perry County. The Carriage Factory tunnels measured 3½ feet wide and 4½ feet high. (Moorehead, Warren K., "Report of Field Work," *Ohio Archaeological & Historical Society Publications*, Vol. VII, 1899, pp 127-128, 132, 137, 142)

MUSKINGUM VALLEY EFFIGY

Near Wilson's Creek, in the Muskingum Valley, an unusual artifact was recovered over a century ago. "A most singular slate effigy was found upon the surface near the semicircle. It is of banded slate 3½ inches long, the upper portion being semicircular, the lower portion having been drawn and narrowed until it gracefully ends in a fair representation of a child's feet and toes. So far as we are aware no effigy of this kind has ever been found in the State of Ohio." (Moorehead, Warren K., *Primitive Man in Ohio*, 1892, p 24)

FRANKLIN COUNTY'S LAST MOUND

An account of demolishing the remaining mound in Columbus was issued in the 1890s. "The last tumulus within the limits of the city of Columbus was explored during August by the Ohio Academy of Science. Originally there were six mounds and two village sites upon the land now covered by the city. ...The mound stood nine feet high, and was 100 feet in diameter at the base. In it were found 27 skeletons and numerous arrow and spear heads, knives, copper beads and pottery sherds." (Editor, "The Ambos Mound," *The Archaeologist*, Vol. 2 No. 10, October 1894, back inside page)

Miami Valley cache

A minor flint cache was found many years ago in Ohio. "During my long period of investigations along archaeological lines I have naturally had some very pleasant surprises, and also some grievous disappointments. Among the former I well remember the first 'cache' of arrow-points I ever found. My father and I were digging out one of the largest poplar stumps on our farm, and in prying out one of the roots imagine my delight in finding several beautiful little white points, all of one form and material. Further careful search revealed 15 in all, and in later plowing over the spot I have found two more of the same form and material. These specimens of fine prehistoric art were directly beneath a very large root and about three feet under ground." (Rayner, John A., "Notes From the Miami Valley," *The Archaeological Bulletin*, May-June 1914, p 35)

Extinct Ohio animals

Everyone is aware that Paleo Indians hunted large game of various kinds, but beyond the huge elephant-like mammals few other extinct types are known. Now, a look at a few of these creatures is possible. Indian Trail Caverns in northwestern Ohio has produced bones dated to at least 9700 BC of four extinct species. Giant beaver bones suggest an animal that weighed up to 450 pounds, while the rare stag-moose had characteristics of both deer and moose. The short-faced bear would have been a formidable predator. Peccaries, pig-like animals, represented the most common bones. While it is not known which of these animals were actually hunted, the Paleo people were likely familiar with them all. (Gnidovec, Dale M., "Bones Tell Animal Tales of Old Ohio," *The Columbus Dispatch*, 3Sept1995)

Prehistoric Ohio exports

Trade in prehistoric times in Ohio worked two ways, bringing artifacts (imported) into the region and sending artifacts (exported) out of the region. An example of the last would be the large Adena knives or blades, usually of Flintridge material. Caches of Adena artifacts have been noted in the states of Delaware, Maryland, New Jersey and Virginia. (Townsend, Earl C., Jr., "Flint Ridge Adena Masterpieces in New Jersey," *The Redskin*, Vol. VIII No. 1, 1973, pp 3-5)

MORGAN COUNTY EXPANDED-NOTCH

One of the best expanded-notch Early Archaic blades from Ohio was found in Morgan County. Made of mixed caramel, cream and dark Upper Mercer flint, the piece was in perfect condition and measured 5 inches long. (Editor, *Ohio Archaeologist*, Vol. 36 No. 2, Spring 1986, front cover and p 3)

POSTCARD EARTHWORKS

Photo-postcards of Ohio mounds and earthworks were popular tourist and chamber of commerce items in the early 1900s. Half a dozen different sites were favorite views. These were: Serpent Mound, Adams County; the Newark Earthworks, Licking County; Cemetery Mound, Marietta; Miamisburg Mound, Montgomery County; Mound City (Hopewell Mound Group), Chillicothe; and, Fort Ancient, Warren County. Undoubtedly other such postcard views exist, and gathering examples could be a collection in itself and a snapshot glimpse of historic Ohio prehistory. (Hothem, Lar, various sources)

OHIO EFFIGY MOUNDS

While being a distant contender in terms of the large number of effigy mounds in Wisconsin, Ohio does have four effigy earthworks. The most famous is the Great Serpent Mound, Adams County, once referred to by some as the "Snake and Egg Mound." There was also another large snake effigy mound in western Ohio, but the head area had been eroded away at an early date. The so-called Alligator Mound (that looks little like an alligator) is also known as the Opossum Mound and is in

Licking County. The Tarlton Cross Mound in southwestern Fairfield County is a sort of geometric effigy. Two other earthworks that have been termed effigy mounds are probably only conjoined smaller mounds in accidentally suggestive forms. One is the Eagle Mound within the Great Circle Earthworks, Licking County. The other is the Tremper Mound, Scioto County, thought to resemble some large, heavy-bodied animal. True effigy mounds seem to be isolated earthworks and not part of any other major earthwork series. (Hothem, Lar, various sources)

EARLY ARCHAIC HUNTING CLUE

Elk bones found on a peat farm near West Liberty (between Bellefontaine and Urbana) were determined to be about 9000 years old. This Mercer County skeleton, recovered in May of 1994, was of interest due to age and rarity, but also because of the condition of a clavicle or collar-bone. It had a hole, suggesting the impact of a projectile point. If so, this indicates hunting by humans in the Early Archaic, ca. 7000 BC. (Associated Press, "Elk Bones Are 9000 Years Old," *The Columbus Dispatch*, 29Jun1995)

LATE WOODLAND CULTURES

One of the lesser-known time periods in Ohio is the post-Hopewell and pre-Mississippian interval. "...in this period of cultural decline in the Ohio Valley—called the Late Woodland period—Ohio had its representatives. Excavations on the Turpin Farm on the Little Miami River near Newtown and at the Merion Site on the Scioto River in Franklin County provide fragmentary evidence of a people with certain Hopewell traits but definitely inferior in the ceremonial aspects of their life and in their construction of burial mounds." (Roseboom, Eugene H. and Francis P. Weisenburger, *A History of Ohio*, Ohio Historical Society, 1953/86, p 10)

RICHLAND COUNTY ADENA BLADE

One of the most exquisite Ohio Adena leaf-shaped blades was formerly in the Dr. Meuser collection. It was found four miles east of Mansfield, Richland County, and the material was Flintridge chalcedony. Length was 10½ inches. (Editor, *The Redskin*, October 1971, pp 140-141)

HARNESS ARTIFICIAL PEARLS

Artificial pearls were found during excavation of the Harness Mound, Ross County, eight miles down the Scioto River from Chillicothe. "Associated with the pearl beads were beads of clay, modeled in exact imitation of the pearls with which they were found. The clay beads were burned and afterward covered with a flexible mica." (Mills, William C., "The Exploration of the Edwin Harness Mound," *Ohio Archaeological & Historical Society Publications*, Vol. XVI, 1907, p 184)

LARGE HOPEWELL BLADE DISTRIBUTION

Hopewell notched blades are frequently found outside the areas of main Middle Woodland occupation in Ohio. "An oddity in distribution of such large (2⅝ x 4½ inches) Hopewell points is that most of the large showy ones are found in the northern half of Ohio rather than in the southern Ohio center of Hopewell activity." (Sarnovsky, John, "A Flint Ridge Hopewell Point," *Ohio Archaeologist*, Vol. 35 No. 2, Spring 1985, p 19)

MIAMI RIVER AXES

The Miami River type axe with the high, narrow, ridged groove and somewhat rectangular blade is almost always 4/4 or full-grooved. However, a small number of 3/4 groove examples exist. (Hothem, Lar, various sources)

81 — Bannerstone, prismoidal type, 1⁷⁄₈ x 2³⁄₁₆ inches. Made of dark brown banded claystone, it is ex-collection Morrow. Brown County. Private collection, Ohio

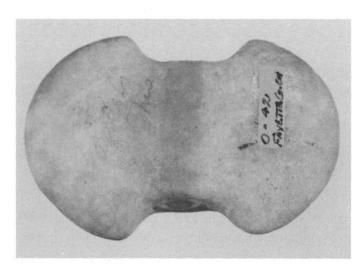

82 — Bannerstone, winged type, 2¹⁄₈ x 3³⁄₁₆ inches. Material is a yellowish quartzite and central drilling was just started. Ex-collection Morrow, this banner is from Fayette County. Private collection, Ohio

83 — Bannerstone, tubular type, 1½x 3¼ inches. This banner was worked in slipped or faulted glacial slate, and the surface is well-polished. Delaware County. Private collection, Ohio

84 — Gorget, spineback type, Glacial Kame people of the Late Archaic, 4⅞ inches long. This beautiful and rare artifact is ex-collections C. Parks and K. Garriot and was found in Williams County. Larry Garvin, **Back to Earth***, Ohio*

85 — Gorget, three-hole Glacial Kame type, 2 x 5 inches. It is made of banded glacial slate and is a scarce type; Lake County. Spahr collection, Ohio

86 — Boatstone, Woodland period, 4⅞ inches long. Current thought on such artifacts is that they were Atl-atl stones. This example in yellow and black hardstone, well-polished, is from Brown County. Spahr collection, Ohio

87 — *Gorget, Woodland period, 5³⁄₈ inches long. Material is banded maroon glacial slate and the artifact is nicely polished. Lucas County. Spahr collection, Ohio*

88 — *Gorget, two-hole, 5¹⁄₂ inches long. Made of banded slate, it also has several lighter-colored inclusions. Allen County. Spahr collection, Ohio*

89 — Gorget, Woodland, 5¾ inches long. Material is banded glacial slate with dark spotting, and the piece is from Portage County. Spahr collection, Ohio

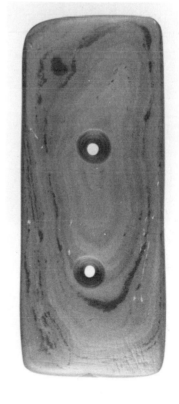

90 — Gorget, banded glacial slate, 2 x 5 inches. Ex-collection Gifford, it is from the Youngstown area of Mahoning County. Spahr collection, Ohio

*91 — Gorget, elliptical type, Adena and Early Woodland period, 5 inches long. The holes are well-centered at each end and the glacial slate has balanced banding and good polish. Lorain County. Larry Garvin, **Back to Earth**, Ohio*

92 — Gorget, biconcave type, 3⅞ inches long. This Adena gorget is made of reddish banded slate and was found in Logan County. Spahr collection, Ohio

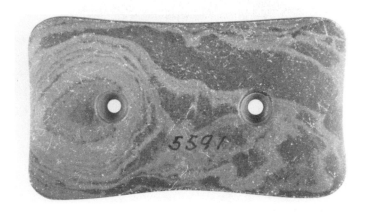

93 — Gorget, Adena quadriconcave, 2⅛ x 3¾ inches. The banded glacial slate has unusual color swirls due to the way the stone was worked. Stark County. Spahr collection, Ohio

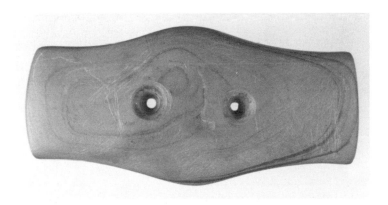

94 — Gorget, Hopewell expanded-center type, 4¼ inches long. This is a scarce type for the Middle Woodland period. Ex-collection Phil Kientz, Monroe County. Spahr collection, Ohio

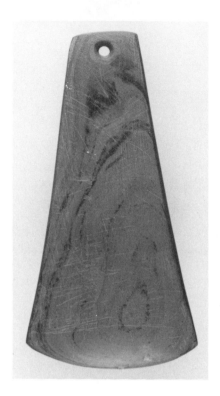

95 — *Pendant, bell-shaped, 3 x 5¾ inches. This fine Woodland piece is ex-collection John B. Kistler and is from Tuscarawas County. Spahr collection, Ohio*

96 — *Pendant, anchor type, Woodland, 1¹⁵/₁₆ x 4¹/₁₆ inches. Material is blue-green banded slate and the surface is very lightly incised with cross-hatched lines. Fairfield County. Lar Hothem collection, Ohio.*

97 — *Pendant, Woodland, 1⅞ x 4¼ inches. From an old collection, this example is made of green banded slate and is from Seneca County. Lar Hothem collection, Ohio*

98 — *Pendant, shield-shape or pentagonal type, 5 inches high. Late Hopewell, of Middle Woodland times, it is well-shaped and polished in a slipped and swirled banded slate; from Miami County. Larry Garvin, **Back to Earth**, Ohio*

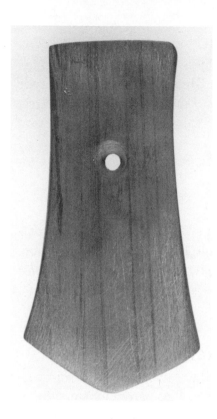

99 — Pendant, Hopewell, 3½ inches high. This Late Hopewell and Middle Woodland example is made of banded slate and has clean and precise lines. Wayne County. Spahr collection, Ohio

100 — Pipe, probably Mississippian period, elbow type, 2 x 3⅝ inches. It is made of very unusual material, mottled brown chlorite, and the pipe surface is highly polished. This rare object is tally-marked on the bowl top. Mahoning County. Private collection, Ohio

BUCK CREEK TYPE CACHE

A cache of four Buck Creek points or blades, Late Archaic / Early Woodland, was found in Ohio prior to 1967. This type has a long, rectangular stem, very barbed shoulders, and fairly straight edge sides. The cache specimens were made of Harrison County (Indiana) flint and were similar in size, from 4⅛ to 4½ inches long. (Editor, *The Redskin*, October 1967, p 136)

OHIO BIRDSTONE QUALITY

Ohio birdstones, of whatever type, tend to be of high quality. Of 30 birdstones shown in the B. W. Stephens collection, 16 or 53% were from Ohio. (Stephens, B. W., *Ohio Archaeologist / Ohio Indian Relic Collectors Society*, Vol. 1 No. 2, July 1951, p 36, back inside cover)

ROSS COUNTY MOUND CACHE

The largest cache of flint artifacts ever found in Ohio was the deposit of Indiana hornstone preforms from Mound No. 2, Hopewell Group, Ross County. The discs were recovered in this manner:

"Excavated from the mound by our men...	7232
Taken out by Squier & Davis...	600
Taken out by Mr. Steel...	200
Given Mr. Hopewell, prior to official count...	80
Found upon the surface near mound afterwards...	42
From other sources ...	31
Total...	8185

"The magnitude of the find surpasses any discovery previously made. They cover a space of 15 x 8 x 3 feet, and weigh nearly 5,000 pounds. It required four horses to haul them from the mound to the camp site." (Moorehead, Warren K., "The Hopewell Group," *The Antiquarian*, Vol. 1 Part 6, June 1897, p 158)

FLINTRIDGE AND VAN PORT

Flintridge material is not limited to the famous quarry sites of southeastern Licking County. Technically, these are flints and cherts of the Van Port member, including the typical chalcedony. Van Port has additional outcrops or quarry sites in Jackson and Muskingum Counties.(Prufer, Olaf, "The Scioto Valley Archaeological Survey," *Studies in Ohio Archaeology*, 1967, p 271) Multi-colored Van Port deposits occur in at least one site in Coshocton County. (Hothem, Lar, *The First Hunters*, 1990, p 102) Van Port thus exists as outcrops or quarries in at least four Ohio counties. The importance here is that when a chalcedony or multi-colored "Flintridge" artifact is found, it did not necessarily come from the Flintridge State Park region in Licking County. It may well have originated at the Van Port quarry nearest the find, wherever that flint source might be located. Coshocton, Licking and Muskingum together form a block of adjoining counties, whereas Jackson County is some distance to the south and slightly to the west. It is not unreasonable to suggest there may be additional outcrops and/or quarries located between these two regions. And, over the years, the descriptive word "Flintridge" has come to mean the material itself, not the exact quarry source. (Hothem, Lar, various sources)

OSAA DONATION

When the Ohio State Archaeological Association met in September of 1875, the members listed donations of prehistoric artifacts that could be seen in the public library at Mansfield, Ohio. One such donation is reprinted here as an example of what was collected almost one and a quarter centuries ago. "Relics on Exhibition / J. P. Henderson, of Richland County, presented the largest and finest collection of the works of the Mound Builders, including polished stone implements of war and of household work; also pipes, idols and images. Together with the more modern hatchets, hammers, spears and arrowheads, gambling apparatus, and other curiosities, almost amounting to hundreds." (*Minutes of the Ohio State Archaeological Convention*, 1875, p 7)

PIPE EYE TREATMENT

The finding of a mound pipe in Pennsylvania may have some bearing on effigy pipes found in Ohio and elsewhere. "...uncovered... was one effigy stone pipe of diorite, having a well defined figure of a wolf or fox. The eye sockets were drilled and filled with some hard white substance, with pupils of black material inserted very artistically and giving the animal a life-like appearance." (Harper, Thomas, "Collector's Department," *The Archaeologist*, Vol. 3 No. 5, May 1895, p 174)

FLINTRIDGE USE

Flintridge is a subject that it is difficult to write too much about and seems to provide endless fascination and attraction. "In the lake region of northern Ohio specimens of this flint are found but in limited numbers. More chalcedony specimens are found here and it would appear as though only this better material was transported through the wilderness that separated the two sections." (Vietzen, Raymond C., *The Ancient Ohioans*, 1946, p 82)

COLLECTING SCIENCE

Writers in the field have long had opinions about collecting prehistoric North American artifacts: "The moral of this 'word with amateur collectors' is that no one should be a mere collector of aboriginal artifacts. The collector must likewise be a student who carefully records the information that chance or diligence unfolds. By means of a little care and study the whole subject will appear in a different and higher light; the collector while satisfying his instinct of acquisitiveness will at the same time become a contributor to the science of archeology, and thus a real benefactor." (Parker, Arthur C., *Archeological History of New York*, Vol. I, No. 89/200, 1922, p 448)

GLACIAL SLATE DISTRIBUTION

Banded slate, the attractive glacial-borne material so often used for prehistoric ornaments, has a somewhat limited distribution. It is common from the Great Lakes to the Ohio River (north to south) and from New York and Pennsylvania to central Illinois (east to west). The raw material came from glacial drift and is found in surface deposits and in the beds of streams. (Weidner, Len, "Banded Slate," *Prehistoric Antiquities Quarterly*, Vol. XIII Qtr. 1, February 1993, p 2)

PREHISTORIC PITS

A few large pits or conical excavations were dug in prehistoric times, and no reasonable purpose for them has ever been advanced. [The author has seen two small examples, one in Coshocton County, one in Fairfield County. Both were from 25 to 30 feet in diameter and both were on hilltops.] The presence of such pits was noted long ago: "In the Scioto Valley, mostly at some distance from other remains, are several excavations which have no counterpart elsewhere; they are not properly enclosures, yet cannot be placed with anything else. On the top of a low hill; near the edge of a terrace in bottom land; or in the middle of a level field; a circular hole has been dug and the earth thrown around the margin. All have been considerably filled in by cultivation, but some are yet from six to eight feet deep and eighty to one hundred and fifty feet in diameter, measuring from the highest part of the wall. The sides now slope uniformly, whatever may have been their original shape, to form an inverted cone; in wet weather they contain some water, which soon disappears. The same end is also effected in a peculiar manner; on a low, depressed ridge connecting two hills, commanded by high ground on every side, a circular embankment has been thrown up to a height of eight feet on so small an area as to leave no level space inside, the inner face of the bank forming a conical basin whose bottom is at the original surface. This form is the last connecting link between the enclosures and the mounds." (Fowke, Gerard, *Geological Survey of Ohio — Archaeology*, 1893, Vol. VII, pp 14-15)

TERMINOLOGY OLD AND NEW

Knowledge and terminology regarding prehistoric artifacts in the Eastern United States, including Ohio, have changed greatly in nearly 100 years. Celts were sometimes called deer skinners, and pecking (as in pecking and grinding) was referred to as picking. Steatite was potstone due to frequent use for such vessels. Long New England slate knives were called bayonet slates, and birdstones were bird amulets; also, birdstones with protruding eyes were said to have projecting ears. Banded glacial slate was sometimes called ribbon stone. (Beauchamp, William M., *Polished Stone Articles Used By the New York Aborigines*, New York State Museum Bulletin, Vol. 4 No. 18, 1897, pp 11, 37, 39, 55, 56, 57, 80)

MOUND CONSTRUCTION AID

An ingenious construction technique was discovered which helped in building the Seip Mound, Ross County, east of Bainbridge. It has long been known that earth was carried in baskets or bags during mound construction, but it would have been quite a climb to near the top of large mounds. For example, at Seip the highest portion was about 20 feet, and other mounds were much higher. "Another feature of the mound was discovered shortly after work was begun on the north side by finding, near the base, several flat stones, averaging from ten to fourteen inches, so placed as to resemble steps. A further examination revealed a series of flat stones, from eighteen to twenty inches under the surface, extending from the base toward the top of the mound. The steps were no doubt used to aid in reaching the summit of the mound with the heavy loads of earth, in the effort of the builders to complete the monument." (Mills, William C., "The Seip Mound," *Putnam Anniversary Volume*, 1909, McGraw reprint, pp 104-105)

GROUND-BREAKING STUDY

Ohio has been in the forefront of archaeological explorations of many kinds. Much groundwork was necessary before Mills' famous *Atlas* was printed, this accomplished of course on a county-by-county basis. The *Atlas* is now a scarce and sought-after book. "In Ohio a plan of work has been adopted that will result in a complete map, giving the position of every aboriginal structure in the State. The original map will be drawn on a large scale, and so accurately constructed that every point of archaeological interest in the state can be indicated within a distance of one hundred yards. ...When completed it will be of incalculable value to science, and to Ohio will belong the honor of having been the first American State to carry out such an undertaking. It is well that this should be the case, for Ohio is especially rich in pre-historic remains, and there is not a county that will not be represented by many mounds or remains of some kind." (Moorehead, Warren K., "Editorial," *The Archaeologist*, Vol. 2 No. 10, October 1894, p 307)

AMERICAN ANTIQUARIAN SOCIETY

Even nearly two centuries ago this state was respected for being a region with gigantic and widespread prehistoric earthworks. "...1812. That was the year in which the American Antiquarian Society was founded, with its primary task to inquire further into the architecture of ancient Ohio." (Kennedy, Roger G., *Hidden Cities — The Discovery and Loss of Ancient North American Civilization*, 1994, p 139)

BUILDING WITH MOUNDS

Mounds in Ohio have suffered strange fates. Some, made partly or entirely of clay were "mined" for this material to make bricks. Early buildings known to have been at least partly constructed from such material include: A church, Belmont County; a courthouse, Franklin County; and, a schoolhouse, Perry

County. Thus, prehistoric structures in a sense live again as historic structures. (Hothem, Lar, various sources)

BONE AWLS AND NEEDLES

Bone tools were made in different ways by several prehistoric cultures in Ohio. "The fashioning of awls from the tarsometatarus of the wild turkey was entirely different in the hands of the two cultures. The Feurt (Fort Ancient, Mississippian period) peoples would use the entire bone, while the Hopewell (Middle Woodland period) would split the bone and make two awls instead of one; again the Feurt people in making a needle would use a flat and long bone, with an eye at one end, and sharp pointed at the other, while the Hopewell peoples in making their needles would use a strong, heavy but small and short bone, round in cross sections, an eye near one end and the other end sharply pointed." (Mills, William C., "The Feurt Mounds and Village Site," *Ohio Archaeological & Historical Society Publications*, Vol. XXVI, 1917, p 333)

SCIOTO VALLEY EARTHWORKS

The Scioto Valley may well have been the most active, in general, of any large United States region in later prehistoric times. "Ohio is noted for its ancient earthworks, and nowhere on the entire North American continent has there been discovered, in an area of like extent, as many prehistoric earthworks as in the Scioto valley. It has been stated that there are, or were, 992 ancient monuments in the valley." (Hopkins, Charles E., *Ohio—The Beautiful and Historic*, 1931, p 18)

ADENA EXPANDED-CENTER GORGETS

In terms of Early Woodland Adena expanded-center gorgets, Ohio has produced many outstanding specimens in size, material and workstyle. Most are of colorful banded slate. (Bartol, F. C., "Expanded Gorgets... Adena Culture," *The Redskin*, April 1969, pp 44-49)

CULTURAL FLINT USE

Certain raw materials seemed to have been preferred during different prehistoric periods in Ohio. "Nellie chert is a 'trademark' for the (Late Paleo) complex, at least in northern Ohio, just as Flint Ridge jewel flint is for Hopewell and the white Flint Ridge flint is for classic Adena." (Smith, Arthur George, "The Sawmill Site, Erie County, Ohio," *Ohio Archaeologist*, Vol. 10 No. 3, July 1960, p 87)

RARE FLINTRIDGE MATERIAL

Perhaps the most unusual variety of Flintridge material (only one example having ever been seen by the author) resembled small, thin, white broken plate fragments floating in honey or amber. The type has been noted before. "Another very interesting deposit of flint, known as the brecciated (or broken) form, was found in the highly colored red flint in this quarry. These deposits are not much larger than a man's fist, are usually oblong in general form, and are made up of small angular fragments of flint which seem to have been held in suspension in clear or slightly colored chalcedony." (Mills, William C., "Flint Ridge," *Ohio Archaeological & Historical Society Publications*, Vol. XXX, 1921, p 117)

SURFACE-HUNTING OHIO

Before about 1950, surface-hunters in Ohio were commonly able to return from an afternoon's hunt with from half a dozen to a dozen undamaged points or blades. Some people in fact did not bother to keep broken or badly damaged artifacts, but let them lay or threw them away. Today, of course, the story is much different. One wonders if the surface-hunters of the year 2050 will look back on these times as the good old days for artifact-hunters. (Hothem, Lar, various sources)

MORROW COUNTY ASHTABULA

An Ashtabula type blade found in Morrow County was called the "Widest flint projectile in Ohio." It was made of light-colored Plum Run flint; width was 4½ inches and length was 6½ inches. (Editor, *Ohio Indian Relic Collectors Society*, Bulletin 24, 1950, pp 32-33)

FAIRFIELD COUNTY EARTHWORK

There was an interesting Hopewell earthwork near Rock Mill, at the Upper Falls of the Hocking (once Hockhocking) River, Fairfield County, Ohio. Known as the Rock Mill Works, it was a square enclosure with two adjoining circles. The square had sides of 420 feet and the largest circular enclosure had a diameter of 210 feet. This was unique, in that it was the only known geometric Hopewell earthwork to be located on a hilltop. (Squier, Ephraim, G. and E. H. Davis, *Ancient Monuments of the Mississippi Valley*, 1847, p 100, plate XXXVI, No. 3)

LICKING COUNTY STONE MOUND

What was probably the second highest mound in Ohio (after the Miamisburg Mound, Montgomery County) once stood in Licking County. Made largely of stone, this mound was located about two miles north of Thornville. In 1831-1832 some fifty wagon teams hauled off many thousand loads. Most of the mound was demolished in order to use the stones for the wall of the Licking County Reservoir. Before it was reduced, the mound was measured to be 189 x 207 feet, and was estimated to be 55 feet high. (Moorehead, Warren K., "Field Work During the Spring and Summer of 1896," *Ohio Archaeological & Historical Society Publications*, Vol. V, 1897, pp 169-170, 172)

PERRY COUNTY LANCEOLATE

An exceptional Late Paleo stemmed lanceolate made of

Flintridge material was found in Perry County, Ohio. Length was 5¾ inches. (Editor, *The Redskin*, April 1968, p 57)

ATHENS COUNTY PALEO POINT

A fine, large Ross County fluted point was found in Athens County. This Early Paleo piece was well-fluted on both lower faces and was made of Harrison County (Indiana) flint. It measured 2 x 5⅜ inches. (Aeh, Gary, "Athens County Fluted Point," *Ohio Archaeologist*, Vol. 19 No. 3, July 1969, p 83)

SMITH/FOWKE

The name of Gerard Fowke, author of the well-known and highly respected *Archaeological History of Ohio*, 1902, was actually a pen name. Mr. Fowke was born Charles Smith in Kentucky in 1849. As he gradually became better known he had difficulty in getting mail due to the number of other individuals named Charles Smith. In 1887 he changed his name, Fowke being his grandmother's maiden name. (*Ohio Indian Relic Collectors Society*, Bulletin No. 16, June 1946)

MOUND ERADICATION

Thousands of mounds and earthworks in Ohio have long been leveled by extensive plowing and agricultural cultivation. Many mounds noted in the early 1800s and recalled by older residents were no longer identifiable as mounds by the early 1900s. In such cases, a century of plowing and cultivation and soil erosion were enough to remove most traces of the average mound. (Hothem, Lar, various sources)

COSHOCTON COUNTY CACHE

A large cache of Adena blades was found in the city of Coshocton in 1963. There were about 330 blades, each 2½ to 8½ inches in length. All were closely spaced together, and on edge. The group was approximately 18 inches in diameter, and the leaf-shaped blades were made of two different materials. One was a hard black flint, the other a dull black material with blue-grey inclusions. This flint probably came from a nearby quarry. (Editor, "Coshocton Adena Cache Blade Find," *Ohio Archaeologist*, Vol. 14 No. 1, January 1964, pp 12-14)

JACKSON COUNTY PETROGLYPHS

The Leo Petroglyphs Site (33JA1) in Jackson County, is one of the state's better-known and best-preserved prehistoric rock art locations. Administered by the Ohio Historical Society and protected by a roofed, rustic shelter, 37 or 38 figures are represented. The rock is a large mass of Black Hand sandstone and the designs were both ground and pecked into the surface. Among the figures depicted are horned entities, humans, birds, fish, generalized animals, and footprints or bear-tracks. An estimate is that the rock art may have been made by the Fort Ancient Indians ca. AD 1300. (Swauger, James L., *Petroglyphs of Ohio*, 1984, pp 98-112)

ICE-AGE LAKE OHIO

During the final stages of the last or Wisconsin Glacier in Ohio, perhaps 12,000 years ago, Paleo hunters never saw Lake Erie. This body of water was created by glacial scooping and at that time was believed to be covered by at least several thousand feet of ice. But Paleo hunters of the Ohio region probably saw a lake no living person today will ever see, Lake Ohio. This enormous body of water was created when glacial ice rammed across the Ohio River in the Cincinnati area, creating a gigantic dam. "…this lake extended up the valley to beyond Pittsburgh, and occupied an area of 20,000 square miles, equal to half that of Ohio." (Howe, Henry citing G. Fredrick Wright, *Historical Collections of Ohio*, Vol. I, 1896, p 99)

DELAWARE COUNTY BIRDSTONE

A fine turtle-type birdstone was found in Delaware County.

Once in the Cameron Parks collection, the artifact had protruding and drilled eyes and an incised mouth. Pictured in Moorehead's *Stone Ornaments* (p 409), the material is banded slate and size is 2½ x 4⅝ inches. (Editor, *The Redskin*, Vol. XIII No. 2, 1978, p 70)

ARCHAIC TOOL CACHES

An interesting detail of Archaic life in the Ohio Valley, at least on river-side sites, may account for the presence of some stone tools. "About every campfire on the middens there is usually to be found a cache of heavy artifacts, made up of several hammerstones, conical or cylindrical pestles, and fully grooved axes. These artifacts seem to have been the household tools used in the preparation of food and in the other activities about the campfire." (Webb, Clarence, "The Archaic Cultures and the Adena People," *Ohio Archaeological & Historical Society Publications*, Vol. LXI, 1952, p 177)

HAMILTON COUNTY ADENA BLADE

One of Ohio's largest stemmed Adena blades was found in Hamilton County. Made of mottled Upper Mercer flint and formerly in the Shipley collection, it measured 9 inches in length. (Shipley, Max, "Flint and Stone From the Max Shipley Collection," *Ohio Archaeologist*, Vol. 23 No. 3, Summer 1973, p 5)

CHIPPED FLINT KNIVES

Chipped artifacts of various Ohio periods, usually referred to rather loosely as projectile points, seem often to have been used as knives. This brings up an interesting question as to how the blades were secured to the shaft or handle. Especially in the Early Archaic, the hafting sections of some examples would seem to be fairly small or short for a secure fit. Type examples for this might be the Lake Erie bifurcate (small) or the Decatur/Fractured Base (short). The Lake Erie would be a small blade with small fit while the Decatur would be a comparatively large blade with short fit. Very possibly attachment was done with a combination of wedging, tying or wrapping, plus an adhesive. Also, many basal dimensions were about right for fitting to an antler handle, which likely provided better support than wood. (Hothem, Lar, various sources)

OHIO CULTURAL DIFFERENCES

Some concise cultural summations can help classify Ohio's prehistoric periods: "Woodland-period peoples were not agriculturists, although they were aware of some domesticated plants. The Late Archaic had much more in common with the Early Woodland than with the Middle Archaic. The Late Woodland period is better understood as the beginning of the Mississippian phase than as the end of the Woodland period. Mississippian societies developed into complex chiefdoms, but did not approach the level of social organization exhibited by the civilizations of Mesoamerica." (Penney, David W.,"Introduction," *Ancient Art of the American Woodland Indians*, 1985, p 12)

PIPES IN OHIO

The Ohio region produced many types of pipes. These include: Curved-base mound; tubular; Iroquoian clay; Iroquoian grotesque bird; biconical; Micmac keel-based; rectangular pipes with birds or animals on the bowl; Monitor; and, bowl and vase-shaped pipes. (McGuire, Joseph D., "Pipes and Smoking Customs of the American Aborigines," *Annual Report of the Smithsonian Institution*, U. S. National Museum, 1897, pp 361-645, plates 1-4)

ADAMS COUNTY SERPENT MOUND

The Serpent Mound has long attracted attention by its size and unique form. "Of all the prehistoric earthworks in North America, the Great Serpent Mound (Adams County) is, as to shape, the most notable." (Groves, G. I., *The Indian Relic Collectors Guide*, 1936, p 21)

OHIO ARCHAIC SITES

Ohio undoubtedly has at least a few deep multi-component sites with comprehensive Archaic layers (8000-1000 BC). Perhaps these sites would be comparable to St. Albans, West Virginia, or Koster, Illinois. With the huge number of Archaic artifacts found, there must have been a heavy prehistoric occupation in that time-period. St. Albans was covered and protected by regular river overflows of silt, and Koster was buried by downwash from bluffs above the site. The question of course is where in Ohio natural water-wash conditions in the past would have been conducive to deeply burying village debris on a periodic basis. (Hothem, Lar, various sources)

SOUTHCENTRAL OHIO EARTHWORKS

Probably the heaviest concentration of earthworks in the state is in southcentral Ohio. This is a rectangular strip about 30 miles wide and 60 miles long, situated north-south. It runs from about the Ross-Pike Counties line north through Pickaway to just south of Columbus in Franklin County. (Mills, William C., *Archeological Atlas of Ohio*, 1914, pp III-IV)

AUGLAIZE COUNTY PICK

One of the longest ceremonial picks (Intrusive Mound people, Late Woodland) was found in Auglaize County. Highly polished, the pick was made of diorite and length was 16½ inches. (Wachtel, H. C., "A Collectors Dream," *Ohio Archaeologist*, Vol. 5 No. 2, April 1955, pp 54-56)

TWO DIFFERENT HIGHBANKS

There are two different and separate Highbanks or High Banks earthworks in Ohio. One is Highbanks (Columbus Metropolitan Park) Works, which overlooks the Olentangy River in southern Delaware County. It is believed to be Late Woodland. Another Highbanks is located a few miles south of

Chillicothe in Ross County. This is (or was) a set of geometric earthworks with associated mounds and parallel walls. It was made by the Hopewell of Middle Woodland times. (Woodward, Susan L. and Jerry N. McDonald, *Indian Mounds of the Middle Ohio Valley*, 1986, pp 60-61; Editor, *Geological Survey of Ohio*, Vol. VII, 1892, p 9, plate III)

UNUSUAL FOOD STORAGE

The prehistoric Indians of Ohio must have been very good at preserving and storing foods for times when the usual supplies were used up or unavailable. An unusual example of such caloric foresight occurred in the Late Archaic period near the north bank of the Ohio River. Excavation of a small campsite revealed a pit dug near water which contained several dozen large clams. The shells were unopened, suggesting the clams were placed in the watery impound while still alive. The only reason for such placement would have been to keep them nearby for later use. (Hothem, Lar, various sources)

LAKE COUNTY HARPOON

An unusual antler harpoon was found at the late prehistoric Reeve Site in Lake County. Made with a single barb, the tool was ¾ inch wide at the base and 6½ inches long. Another, smaller antler harpoon came from Erie County and had two barbs on one side. (Vietzen, Raymond C., *The Immortal Eries*, 1945, pp 267-268, figure 87)

BUCKEYE LAKE EXPEDITIONS

A considerable prehistoric artifact collection was put together by a gentleman from Pennsylvania during the Great Depression of the 1930s. Each spring of the year he would ride a train from Aliquippa to Columbus, Ohio, with several large baggage containers. These held food and camping gear; he would next hitch a ride east to the Buckeye Lake region, once known as the Great Swamp. Then the man spent up to a month there, camping at different places and surface-hunting fields from dawn to dusk. He also purchased, for small amounts, artifacts found by Buckeye Lake area farmers. (Hothem, Lar, personal communication)

INTRUSIVE MOUND STONE HEADS

Among the rarest and most mysterious artifacts from Ohio are the large, carefully sculpted stone heads. These seem to be associated with the Late Woodland Intrusive Mound people. The heads are oval in shape, with a flattened back. Eyes are deep-set, and the nose and eyebrows accented, the mouth relatively small and in triangular line with the nose. Two examples have come from Ross and Scioto Counties. These are sometimes called masks, but their original purpose is unknown. (Editor, "A Human Head Effigy," *Ohio Archaeologist*, Vol. 21 No. 2, Spring 1971, p 8; Converse, Robert, "The Heinisch Mound Human Head Effigy," *Ohio Archaeologist*, Vol. 38 No. 2, Spring 1988, p 21; Museum, Mound-Builder State Memorial, Newark, Ohio)

UNUSUAL HOPEWELL ARTIFACTS

Highly unusual artifacts were found in the Hopewell Group of mounds in Ross County, on the North Fork of Paint Creek: Stone dishes, large discs of flint, large obsidian blades, quartz crystal artifacts, and many decorative designs in sheet copper. (Shetrone, Henry C., "Explorations of the Hopewell Group...," *Ohio Archaeological & Historical Society Publications*, Vol. XXXV, 1926, p 226)

SQUIER AND DAVIS EXPORT

How the Squier and Davis collection (with much rare Ohio material) went to the Blackmore Museum in England: "This was the finest Collection of its kind in the United States, and it is doubtful whether one of equal extent, and so rich in the works of primitive man in America, can again be made; indeed, many of the specimens are unique. This unrivalled [sic] Collection was offered to several of our Antiquarian and Historical Societies; but, Mr. Blackmore, being in this country, in 1863, and learning that the owner was anxious to sell it, became its purchaser. Mr. Blackmore told me that he felt very reluctant to remove the Collection from the United States, where he thought it should remain, and it was not until he had been assured that the Societies to which it had been offered had declined buying it, that he concluded to take it." (Stevens, Edward T., "Preface to the American Edition," *Flint Chips*, 1870, pp XIX-XX)

HANCOCK COUNTY LANCEOLATE

A superior Late Paleo unstemmed lanceolate was found in Hancock County. The material was grey Upper Mercer flint, and length was 6¼ inches. (Editor, *Ohio Archaeologist*, Vol. 23 No. 3, Summer 1973, p 24)

EARLY OHIO AGRICULTURE

Farming in Ohio may go back more years than is usually known, as indicated in Lorain County: "...the Leimbach Site is one of the most ancient localities in the Great Lakes which has preserved evidence of agriculture, albeit of probably the most marginal type. The presence of squash seeds at this place and also at the Schultz Site in Michigan has been independently dated by radiocarbon assay to the sixth century B. C." (Mason, Ronald J., *Great Lakes Archaeology*, 1981, pp 229-230)

AN OLD STORY

For those who remark about the large number of Ohio artifact collectors who walk the fields and surface-hunt today, here are a few words from ninety years ago: "In all parts of the state, but especially along the principal rivers artificial objects of stone are found in such numbers as to astonish collectors and students. Year after year, the same fields yield their tribute to the cabinet; every forest cleared away, every old meadow put in cultivation, opens up a new source of supply. With each successive plowing, relics in sufficient numbers to stimulate further research are brought to light on village-sites which keen-eyed collectors have scanned until it would seem not a flake could be left." (Fowke, Gerard, *Archaeological History of Ohio*, 1902, pp 509-510)

FULTON COUNTY CACHE

A superb Adena blade, one of a cache of 252, was found in Fulton County sometime in the early 1900s. Made of high-grade jewel translucent Flintridge material, the blade was 7³⁄₁₆ inches long. (Editor, *Ohio Archaeologist*, Vol. 28 No. 2, Spring 1978, back cover)

SEIP MOUND FABRIC

Regarding samples of textiles taken from the Seip Mound (Hopewell, near Bainbridge, Ross County), various pieces of fabric were recovered, including an advanced form of weaving: "...a very fine reticulated weaving was frequently met with. The warp in this textile was placed about one-eighth of an inch apart and the woof one-sixteenth of an inch and the yarn finely spun." (Mills, William C., "Explorations of the Seip Mound," *Ohio Archaeological & Historical Society Publications*, Vol. XVIII, 1909, pp 316-317)

ROSS COUNTY NATURAL CURIOSITIES

In Paint Creek, near Spruce Hill Fort or hilltop enclosure in Ross County, several early authorities reported the presence of Indian wells in the creek bed. They described them as being deep, circular, filled with gravel and covered with a stone cap that often had a hole in the center. However, later and more scientific examination indicated that the large depressions were not wells at all but were natural features called septaria. These are calcite-filled openings in other rock formations, typically shale or slate layers. The lids or covers were parts of the deposits that remained because they had not been dissolved by water. (Squier, Ephraim G. and E. H. Davis, *Ancient Monuments of the Mississippi Valley*, 1848, p 13)

OHIO BALL-TYPE BANNERS

Ball bannerstones, usually made of colorful banded slate and almost always grooved or fluted, were popular in Archaic times in Ohio. Of 21 specimens from an Indiana collection, 12 or 57% were from Ohio. (Bartol, Fred, *Ohio Archaeologist / Ohio Indian Relic Collectors Society*, July 1951, pp 20-21)

ARCHAIC LIZARD EFFIGIES

Lizard or effigy stones may date from the Middle Archaic and were probably associated with the Atl-atl. Ranging in length from 3 to 7 inches, most are about 5 inches. The traditional effigy has a flattened bottom, and a shortened head region which expands, sometimes abruptly, to form an elongated body-like section. This in turn tapers to a long tail section. Many effigies of this type have been found in Ohio, especially in the western portion. All tend to have smooth, flowing lines and some have rudimentary eyes or mouths. The foremost collector of these mysterious objects in the past was Dr. Gordon Meuser, who possessed over one hundred. (Hothem, Lar, various sources)

UPPER OHIO VALLEY ARCHAIC

Southeastern Ohio, despite a general shortage of major prehistoric sites, was evidently part of a key location. "The Upper Ohio Valley has been the path of movements of many peoples over long periods of time. It is the natural gateway and most direct route to the northeast from the Mississippi and Ohio Valleys. Thus, Archaic assemblages of the Upper Ohio Valley have important relationships with manifestations in surrounding areas in eastern North America." (Dragoo, Don, *Archaic Hunters of the Upper Ohio Valley*, 1959, p 215)

PICKAWAY COUNTY MICA SHEET

An early writer reported that a large Circleville mound produced a sheet of mica that was, at least by Ohio standards, huge. While mica is fairly common in Ohio Hopewell mounds, this particular piece was 3 feet long, 1½ feet wide and 1½ inches thick. Assuming the sheet was at least generally worked to those dimensions, this means it was probably the largest non-earthwork prehistoric artifact found in Ohio, other than an occasional dugout wooden water craft. Also, since the origin of mica is assumed to be in the southern Appalachian Mountains and the mica had to be transported here, the sheet gives some idea of what sort of load could be brought along the early trade routes. Of course there is no way of knowing whether such a load was large, small or average. (Shepherd, Henry A., *Antiquities of the State of Ohio*, 1887, p 104)

BAUM VILLAGE FISH-HOOKS

Bone fish-hooks were common in the refuse pits of Fort Ancient village sites. They were made primarily from two sources, deer and wild turkeys. Hooks were found in different manufacturing stages, from little-worked sections of bone to complete and polished artifacts. Hooks were unbarbed but some had a knob at the upper end for line attachment; none were eyed. Cutting the bone carefully at an angle resulted in an elongated oval. This in turn was carefully cut in two places to produce two hooks. (Mills, William C., "Fish-Hooks Found at the Baum Village Site," *Ohio Archaeological & Historical Society Publications*, Vol. IX, 1901, pp 520-523)

GREENE COUNTY DRILL

One of the finest drills ever found in Ohio was probably made from an Archaic notched-base blade, as indicated from the remaining base on the drill. It was found near Oldtown, Greene County, in 1885. Made of grey Wyandotte flint (Indiana hornstone), the drill was formerly in the collection of Arthur

Altick. It was 5½ inches long, very well-made and perfectly balanced. (Grimm, Robert E., *Prehistoric Art*, 1953, pp 52-53)

BIRDSTONES WITH EYE-BANDING

Slate birdstones with banding which forms an eye-like configuration in the head region are uncommon: "Standing among the royalty in the birdstone kingdom is the natural eye variety. The name is used to describe the correct positioning of the natural stone markings that form a circular or ovate shape of an eye. Its rarity is attested by the fact that among more than 1000 birdstones, 7.5% are of the natural eye variety—one in every 13." (Tiell, William,"The Natural Eye Birdstone," *Ohio Archaeologist*, Vol. 25 No. 4, Fall 1975, p 4)

OHIO EARTHWORKS

About Ohio's Woodland-period earthworks: "The ancient earth works of Ohio, in their variety, magnitude and extent, excel those of all the other States. Single mounds of greater size are found elsewhere, but no other State has such a variety of these works, or such numbers of them as Ohio." (Read, M. C., *Archaeology of Ohio*, 1888, p 79)

ROCK-SHELTER FISHNET

Many rare and normally perishable artifacts have been found in the dry rock-shelters of southern Ohio. One object, from Indian Cave (Canter's Caves, Jackson County), was a section of fishnet. It measured 16 x 18 inches and the square meshes were ⅜ inch a side. The thread had been made from swamp milkweed. The size of the mesh suggests that very small fish could be taken. (Shetrone, Henry C., "Some Ohio Caves and Rock Shelters," *Ohio Archaeological & Historical Society Publications*, Vol. XXXVII, 1928, pp 13, 15-16)

RARE HOPEWELL ARTIFACTS

Warren K. Moorehead, excavating in 1891-92 at the

Hopewell Group in Ross County, found many museum quality artifacts. Several of them may be unique in Ohio prehistory due to the combination of metals in individual artifacts. The major example would be ear spools made of meteoric iron, with a layer of copper on one side and silver on the other. (Hertzog, Keith P., "Hopewell Meteoric Iron Artifacts," *Ohio Archaeologist*, Vol. 15 No. 1, January 1965, p 9)

OHIO SANDIA-LIKE POINTS

Sandia points have long been an enigma, with some students even wondering about the existence of such pre-Clovis points or blades. Others have fewer questions. "Seemingly true Sandias have been reported from Alberta, Canada, and Geauga County, Ohio, the latter from a surface collection made about 1910. Doubtless there are more that might be recorded." (Brennan, Louis A., *American Dawn*, 1970, p 18)

MOUNDS AND COMMUNICATIONS

We know very little about prehistoric communications over distance, what might or might not have been possible: "...there is little doubt that the Mound-builders in the latter period of their occupancy of this (southcentral Ohio) region, when apprehensive of danger from their enemies, employed a system of signal telegraph by which communication was had, through means of the watch-fire or torch, between localities as distant as those now occupied by Cincinnati and Dayton. Only a few minutes were necessary by means of such a perfected system in which to transmit a signal fifty or one hundred miles. (Short, John T., *The North Americans of Antiquity*, 1882, p 52)

COSHOCTON COUNTY POTTERY

In the mid-19th century an unusual pottery vessel was found in Ohio. "In the year 1850, in digging a well, Isaac Stull, near his residence, half a mile south of the village of Orange, about 5 feet below the surface, came upon an earthen vessel that would hold, perhaps, about two gallons. Before discovering this relic he unfortunately stepped upon and broke it. It was found mouth upward, and resembled in many respects a two-gallon crock. The rim around the top was artistic, and intended to aid in lifting the vessel. It was formed of a bluish earth, and seemed to have been subjected to heat. It was ornamented all over the exterior by finely pulverized white flint, somewhat resembling rice-grains, which adhered firmly to it. A short time afterward, in plowing in a field northwest of his house, Mr. Stull turned up a fragment of the same kind of vessel, as large as his hand." (Hill, George W., "Ancient Earthworks of Ashland County, Ohio / Ancient Earthworks in Ohio," *Annual Report of the Board of Regents of the Smithsonian Institution / 1877*, 1878, p 264)

FIRES AT HILLTOP ENCLOSURES

The presence of cinders and burned earth at some of the Hopewellian hilltop enclosures suggests that at some distant time wooden structures were burned, perhaps denoting successful attacks on defensive earthworks. Such charred remains have been found at Spruce Hill (Ross County), Foster's Crossing (Warren County), and Fort Miami (Hamilton County). (Prufer, Olaf, "The Hopewell Complex of Ohio," *Hopewellian Studies*, Vol. XII, 1970, pp 68-69)

PREHISTORIC PEOPLES OF OHIO

A general partition of the four major prehistoric periods in Ohio (Eastern Midwest) includes a large number of prehistoric sub-divisions. Pre-Paleo sites may exist, these being perhaps 14,000 BC or earlier. Early (Clovis) followed by Late (Lanceolate) Paleo comes down to ca. 8000 BC. The Archaic (Early, Middle and Late) terminates with Glacial Kame. Adena (Early Woodland times) begins ca. 1000 BC, and Red Ochre may have co-existed with Adena. Middle Woodland (Hopewell) and Late Woodland (Intrusive Mound and Cole) round out the Woodland, ending ca. AD 800-1000. Mississippian times had Ft.

Ancient in southern Ohio, plus Sandusky and Whittlesey in northern Ohio. The groups and sub-groups are often further separated into smaller divisions with differing traits. (Hothem, Lar, various sources)

LIDDED POTTERY

Most of the pottery vessels found in Ohio had open tops, but a lidded or covered pottery container was once noted: "In another mound in Ohio, a curiously ornamented urn, having a capacity of six quarts, was found. It had a cover which fitted down over the vessel for six inches." (King, Blanche Busey, *Under Your Feet*, 1939, p 97)

COSHOCTON COUNTY FLINT QUARRIES

While much has been written about the famous Flintridge (Van Port) quarries in Licking County, less is known about the actual quarries of Coshocton County (Upper Mercer). Known variously as "Coshocton," "Ohio Blue," or Warsaw flint, these quarries were a major prehistoric material source. A description of them was done over fifty years ago. "One of the most interesting places in Jefferson Township is the ridge about two miles southeast of the village of Warsaw. ...the first thing that attracts the attention of the visitor to this place is the large number, size, and shape of the excavations. Covering an area of several hundred acres are numerous excavations on this ridge, varying from ten to twenty feet in width and from fifty to one hundred feet in length. The depth varies but little (from ten to twelve feet), in each case reaching down to the layer of flint rock. This layer of flint rock perhaps does not exceed two feet in thickness. ...the flint found in this area is of a superior quality, found in only a few other places in Ohio. ...these mines are still worked for the quartz they produce. The articles made from this rock vary in color, being white, blue, amber, black and mixed hues." (Nowels, G. P., *Historical Collections / Warsaw and Walhonding Valley*, L. C. Shaw, Ed., 1934, p 77)

KNOBBED LUNATE DISTRIBUTION

Knobbed lunates are rare and graceful Archaic bannerstones that apparently have a limited distribution. "An interesting observation on ultimate design knobbed lunates is the fact that most of them were found in a relatively small area centering around Delaware County, Indiana and the adjacent Darke County, Ohio. The ones that were not found in these two counties were found only one or two counties away on both sides of the Ohio and Indiana state lines." (Edwards, Beth and David, "Knobbed Lunate Bannerstone from Delaware County, Indiana," *Prehistoric America*, Vol. 24 No. 4, 1990, p 26)

MOOREHEAD'S MISCONCEPTION

An early summary of work on Ohio's prehistory is worthy of thought, if not outright acceptance. "The labors of these gentlemen [Squier and Davis, *Ancient Monuments of the Mississippi Valley*, 1847] brought the mounds of the state of Ohio to the attention of persons both home and abroad. As a natural result museums, institutions and private individuals have worked in the Ohio field almost continuously for fifty years and the story of Ohio archaeology is written. ...It is not so much that Ohio is a richer field than Missouri, Tennessee, Illinois or Arizona, but that it is well nigh exhausted." (Moorehead, Warren K., *Prehistoric Implements*, 1900, p 330)

ROSS COUNTY PALEO POINT

A large unfluted-fluted point was found near Chillicothe. Chipped from a brown and tan flint, the Paleo artifact was just over 5 inches long. (Shirley, Dave, "Two Flint Artifacts," *Ohio Archaeologist*, Vol. 38 No. 4, Fall 1988, p 36)

TREMPER MOUND MATERIALS

In addition to the usual copper ear-spools or ear-ornaments found in major Hopewell mounds in southern Ohio, Tremper Mound (near the Scioto River, Scioto County) had artifacts made of other materials. At the Tremper Mound, a pair of ear-spools was made of highly polished black Ohio slate and had a maximum diameter of 2⅛ inches. Another pair was made of light red pipestone, and these artifacts were 1⅝ inches in diameter. (Mills, William C., "Exploration of the Tremper Mound," *Ohio Archaeological & Historical Society Publications*, Vol. XXV, 1916, pp 375-376)

OHIO VALLEY WATERSHED

The importance of the Ohio River to prehistoric Ohio cultures has often been assumed but has not been frequently mentioned in the literature. "Along the stream itself one may discern, on both north and south bank sites, all kinds of cultures, thus proving that the Ohio River was not only a thoroughfare but *the* thoroughfare in prehistoric times. It is only when one proceeds up the streams from the Ohio bank fifty or a hundred miles in Illinois, Kentucky, Indiana, and Ohio that one observes how the local cultures have developed. The culture of the Muskingum and Scioto in Ohio are practically the same; the Miami is different." (Moorehead, Warren K., *The Stone Age in North America*, Vol. II, 1910, p 360)

SCIOTO COUNTY WALLS

The parallel walls associated with the Hopewell earthworks at Portsmouth were possibly the most sophisticated in the state. One line of walls went to the Ohio River (and apparently resumed on the Kentucky bank), another set also went to the Ohio at a closer distance, while a third extended into the hills toward the Scioto River. The walls were about 160 feet apart, were from 1½ to 4 feet high, and averaged 2½ feet high. Total length of the parallel walls was about eight miles. (Shepherd, Henry A., *Antiquities of the State of Ohio*, 1887, p 55)

ALL ARTIFACTS IMPORTANT

While Ohio people continue to donate prehistoric artifacts

to museums, for these artifact groupings to have real and ongoing scientific value they should not be slanted or limited by only what the collector desires or deems worthy. "...The museums are full of axes, celts, pipes, banner stones, discoidals, hematites, tubes, slate ornaments and ceremonials, pestles, hammers, etc. What the museums need (as of great value to Archaeological Science) are collections from a single locality including *everything* found in that locality. They want the finds of the village site, the studies in unfinished specimens, the poor and the good, the imperfect as well as the perfect. In this regard the collectors make a great error. Most of them do not save *everything* but cling to the 'pretty relics' and discard the rough and the rude. Personally, I would give more for a collection, provided it contained *all* the types, *all* the finds of a certain valley than for just the fine, perfect objects of that valley. From a collection of the latter I would be misled, for, if I accepted it as indicative of the people of that valley, I would say that they made most beautiful works of aboriginal art, nothing rude or unfinished being turned out by their artisans. In such a statement I would be unpardonably wrong." (Moorehead, Warren K., "Information for Collectors," *The Archaeologist*, Vol. 2 No. 2, February 1894, p 56)

Ross County drill

One of the longest drills or flint pins to come from the state of Ohio was made of blue and white (probably Upper Mercer) material and was found in Ross County. It was ⅛ inch across at the base and was 6½ inches long. (Editor, *The Redskin*, July 1966, p 16)

Exploring rivers

Warren K. Moorehead rarely wrote about his personal feelings, but about some of his experiences in Ohio he did put them on paper. "To me the most interesting part of archaeology is work in the field, and the comparison of the remains or art forms of one river valley with those of another. The only way to obtain a correct and comprehensive idea of the archaeology of a valley is to follow the main stream from source to mouth. This must be done personally. One cannot obtain an adequate idea through the reports, by maps, or by visiting two or three localities on the river. I have always thought that the most satisfactory (to myself) work that I ever did was the following of the Muskingum, Scioto and Little Miami rivers from their smallest streams to their mouths." (Moorehead, Warren K., *Prehistoric Implements*, 1900, p 363)

MOUND CONFIGURATIONS

The shape of Ohio mounds is sometimes a clue to their origin. "While the mounds of the Hopewell culture often are irregular in shape, those of the Adena type usually are distinguished by their symmetry, often approaching as nearly to the figure of a cone as is practical to construct from loose earth. In this respect the mounds of the Fort Ancient peoples are intermediate, their form being conical, but as a rule they are not so carefully constructed as the Adena mounds. (Shetrone, Henry C., "The Indian in Ohio," *Ohio Archaeological & Historical Society Publications*, Vol. XXVII, 1919, p 497)

ADENA DUCK PIPES

At least two images or effigies of the shoveler duck in the form of Adena tubular pipes have been found in Ohio. One was found in the 1930s near Dayton, in the Englewood Mound. The second, the Ludwick Pipe, was found about 1944 in a mound on the Duncan farm in Highland County. Made of Ohio pipestone in mottled grey, the effigy includes the bill, head and neck regions. Overall, the damaged specimen measures 5¾ inches long. (Baby, Raymond, "An Adena Effigy Pipe," *Ohio Archaeologist*, Vol. 19 No. 1, January 1969, pp 16-17)

LAKE COUNTY CALCITE PIPES

The northern area of Ohio was an important pipe-making

region. A late prehistoric site near Willoughby, Lake County, Ohio, has produced some unusual pipes. "One of the outstanding features of this site is the finding of pipes made of crystal calcite. This is very beautiful when worked and resembles quartz to a great extent. This calcite is a native material in Lake County." (Vietzen, Raymond C., *Ancient Man in Northern Ohio*, 1941, p 13)

OHIO PIPESTONE COMPOSITION

Many years ago, a professor Church of the Royal Agriculture College, England, made an analysis of the Ohio pipestone material in the Tremper Mound pipes, which pipes went to the Blackmore Museum in England. The technical report, in part, read: "This stone is not a definite mineral but a mixture of minerals—a rock. Its hardness varies in different parts of the same specimen—the harder parts approaching six and the softer parts not exceeding 4.5. These softer parts are paler in colour, contain much less iron than the harder parts, and seem to consist of minute globules of a compound silicate, perhaps a feldspar. Some of the pipes and other objects fashioned from this ferruginous stone are much fissured internally and blacker inside than out. When most compact this stone has a density 4.3; when least so about 3.07. ...The collection contains many examples of this curious clay ironstone. Some of these approach in structure to the red pipestone (Coteau des Prairies), often termed catlinite. But they are more variolitic in texture and much more mottled and diversified in colour. Some specimens are iron grey or dark brown; others pale grey, spotted with white." (Mills, William C., "Exploration of the Tremper Mound," *Certain Mounds and Village Sites in Ohio*, Vol. II, 1917, p 132)

POSSIBLE PREHISTORIC DAM

While one can read nearly endless accounts of prehistoric earthworks of one kind or another in Ohio, hardly anything has been written, or known, about ancient water works. An early account of Fort Hill, Highland County, does make such an allusion. "A short distance below Bragg's Tannery, on a small stream which is fed by a number of fine springs, there seems to have been a dyke [sic] thrown across the stream, which would form a lake of considerable extent in the basin-shaped valley." (Overman, Henry W., "Fort Hill, Ohio," *Ohio Archaeological & Historical Society Publications*, Vol. I, 1887-88, p 260)

EARLY SOCIETY

The first meeting of the pre-Archaeological Society of Ohio collecting and scientific group is here described: "On a Saturday afternoon, March 14th, 1942 a small group of active Indian relic collectors met at the Ohio State Museum to form the Ohio Indian Relic Collectors Society. From this embryonic stage it progressed to a growing organization of 200 members." (Vietzen, Raymond C., "Just Reminiscing," *Ohio Indian Relic Collectors Society*, Bulletin No. 18, June 1947)

FLINTRIDGE WORK TERMINATION

The famous Flintridge quarries of southeastern Licking County are known to have been worked since Early Paleo times, ca. 9500 BC. There has been very little information as to when such mining work stopped at the quarries. There is, however, one hint. "No reference to Flint Ridge and its pits can be found among the earliest travelers and explorers. ...Explorations indicate that there has been no quarrying at Flint Ridge in the last four or five centuries." (Moorehead, Warren K., "Collecting at Flint Ridge," *A Narrative of Explorations in New Mexico, Arizona, Indiana, Etc*, 1906, p 109)

EARLY WOODLAND BIRDSTONES

Wide, flat, rounded, birdstone-like effigies with small heads may be relatively late in prehistory. Such effigies are quite rare; the drilling may give a clue as to their origin in time. "Features include two holes drilled in typical 'Adena style' from the underside of the effigy, and a small tapered head and eyes, again suggesting a lizard or its close relative." (Gehlbach, Don, "The Enigmatic 'Birdstone,'" *Ohio Archaeologist*, Vol. 36 No. 3, Summer 1986, p 21)

LIZARD EFFIGY DISTRIBUTION

The Dr. Meuser collection as evidenced in the auction catalog contained some 178 lizard or effigy stones, the largest such type grouping made. Probably Middle Archaic in origin, almost all the effigies were made of glacial slate except for two granite specimens. These were from Erie and Van Wert Counties, respectively. Six specimens were listed only as having an Ohio origin, but the remainder were provenanced to the county level. The top effigy-producing counties were: Delaware, 17; Warren, 13; Miami, 10; Ross, 8; Clermont and Sandusky, 7 each; and, Franklin, Hancock, Morrow and Preble Counties with 6 each. And although effigy stones are listed as coming from a total of 49 Ohio counties, a western Ohio distribution is obvious. (Garth's Auction Barn, Inc., *Indian Relic Collection from the Estate of Dr. Gordon F. Meuser of Columbus, Ohio*)

HOPEWELL AND HEATED COPPER

New or at least different glimpses of Ohio's prehistory can sometimes come from surprising sources. While it is generally agreed that the Hopewell people never smelted copper or poured mould-made objects in this metal, an early report at least suggests that some individuals in this culture would have observed copper melting and realized that copper had this property. "Numerous mortuary altars have been found in the older mounds covered with articles of copper which, having been sacrificed in fire, were fused together in many instances, and in some cases were so thoroughly melted as to form almost homogeneous masses." (Cushing, Frank H., "Primitive Copper Working: An Experimental Study," *The Archaeologist*, Vol. 2 No. 4, April 1894, p 102)

OCCUPIED ROCK-SHELTERS

Rock overhangs or rock-shelters exist in sandstone regions of Ohio, yet no major summary of them has been done; likely most large shelters would prove to have had at least some occupation. "Caves adapted to human habitation are very rare in Ohio, but rock shelters, which would afford protection from the weather, are abundant. These have been very inadequately explored. Every rocky projection under which a benighted hunter would seek protection, if there is a dry surface below it, will, on examination, show evidences of human habitation, and sometimes of a habitation greatly prolonged." (Read, M. C., "Rock Shelters," *Archaeology of Ohio*, 1888, p 56)

DIFFICULTY OF FLINTRIDGE QUARRYING

Prehistoric flint-mining or quarrying in Ohio was not always an easy, or even possible task. "The next quarry of special interest was No. 3. This quarry is located not far from the outcrop along the cleared field on the Coal Company's property, perhaps a little more than half a mile directly north-east from the blacksmith-shop. The pit was seventeen feet long and fifteen feet wide, and at no point in the quarry had the bottom of the flint been reached. Near the center of the quarry, to the west, a projection of flint extended almost across the quarry. Examination showed that the deposit was a very compact variety of yellow flint, practically devoid of seams, which baffled our own efforts in quarrying with our modern chisels and hammers. We were very desirous of securing large samples of this highly-colored flint, and preparing the stone for a charge of dynamite, were able to secure good specimens of both yellows and reds. Many instances exist on the "Ridge" where the ancient quarryman was compelled to abandon the removal of fine flint, owing to the absence of cracks or other defects which would enable him to work through to the base of the deposit, and thus gain a vantage point for further procedure." (Mills, William C., "Flint Ridge," *Ohio Archaeological & Historical Society Publications*, Vol. XXX, 1921, pp 117-119)

Index

159

164